IMAGES
of Sport

WOLVERHAMPTON WANDERERS FOOTBALL CLUB

IMAGES
of Sport

WOLVERHAMPTON WANDERERS FOOTBALL CLUB

Geoff Allman

TEMPUS

Frontispiece: The Wolves team of 1921.

First published 2002
Copyright © Geoff Allman, 2002

Tempus Publishing Limited
The Mill, Brimscombe Port,
Stroud, Gloucestershire, GL5 2QG

ISBN 0 7524 2427 0

TYPESETTING AND ORIGINATION BY
Tempus Publishing Limited
PRINTED IN GREAT BRITAIN BY
Midway Colour Print, Wiltshire

Contents

PRICE - - TWOPENCE.

OFFICIAL PROGRAMME

OF

WOLVERHAMPTON WANDERERS FOOTBALL CLUB (1923) LIMITED

SEASON 1946-1947

Directors :

Chairman - J. S. BAKER, Esq.

J. EVANS, Esq., C. H. HUNTER, Esq., B. MATTHEWS, Esq.,
A. H. OAKLEY, Esq., J.P.

Secretary-Manager: E. T. VIZARD.   Assistant-Secretary: J. T. HOWLEY.
Telephone: 24053/4.   Telegrams: " Wanderers," Wolverhampton.

62 PRACTICE MATCH *37*

COLOURS. 6.

v.

WHITES. 0.

SATURDAY, AUGUST 24th, 1946.

KICK OFF 3 P.M.

FOOTBALL AT MOLINEUX GROUNDS

FOOTBALL LEAGUE - DIVISION I

Match No. I

ARSENAL *v.* WOLVES

Saturday Next, August 3lst, 1946.

Kick-off 3 p.m.

Reserved Seats for this match will be on sale at the Office, Waterloo Road, from Monday next.

WATERLOO ROAD CENTRE STAND	....	6/- (Inc. Tax)
MOLINEUX STREET CENTRE STAND	....	4/6 (Inc. Tax)
WATERLOO ROAD WING STANDS	....	4/- (Inc. Tax)

Paulton Brothers, Printers, Berry Street, Wolverhampton.

This match programme from the public practice match at the start of the 1946/47 season introduced Wolves fans to their new signings, including two of the greatest players in their history: Jesse Pye, the striker from Notts County, and Johnny Hancocks, the winger from Walsall.

Introduction

It was during the dark days of the early years of the Second World War that my infant heart thrilled to the radio commentaries of the late great Raymond Glendenning. Long before I actually saw a game of football, I pictured what was happening in those wartime games in my mind's eye. Then on 15 January 1944 my dad took me to Molineux to see a Wolves v. Coventry game.

I can still recall the thrill of Arnold Stephens banging home the opening goal for Wolves and Jimmy Dunn restoring that lead after Coventry had equalised. The game ended 2-2, and fans went away complaining about the 'two gift goals' that lapses by Wolves 'keeper Don Bilton had presented to the visitors; I, on the other hand, took away memories that have lasted a lifetime – the heading ability of Stan Cullis, the fiery temper of Spanish striker Emilio Aldecoa, the overlapping of pre-war full-back Frank Taylor and many, many more.

Since then, I have been amongst the 50,765 who saw Wolves so narrowly miss out on the first League Championship after the war when beaten by Liverpool in May 1947, but I have also been amongst the 97,886 who saw Wolves win the League Cup final against the odds in 1974, when a hobbling Dave Wagstaff somehow crossed the ball for John Richards – who was also operating virtually on one leg – to bang home the winner against Manchester City.

I have been lucky enough to see Wolves win three League Championships and shared the agony of three successive relegation seasons. I have been at Molineux with only just over 2,000 others as both the team and the ground seemed to be falling apart in the mid-1980s, but I have also seen the glorious resurrection of both ground and team as that decade gave way to the 1990s. Shall I see Wolves in the Premiership? I hope so, but in any event nothing can take away the memories, just a fraction of which are recaptured in the following pages.

Here's hoping that readers will be enabled to relive their own memories and perhaps learn of a few other personalities in the history of Wolves that they may not have heard of before.

Acknowledgements

I am indebted to so many who have helped and encouraged me in this labour of love, particularly James Howarth and staff of Tempus Publishing, the *Express & Star* and Don Stanton of Pemandos Publishing for permission to use photographs, Mike Bondy for his tireless research into newspapers of a hundred and more years ago, Jim Evans for loan of items from his peerless collection of Wolves memorabilia and my wife, Judith, who has given tremendous secretarial support – frequently when not properly match fit. Finally, thanks to all of those who have helped to keep Wolves alive and vibrant from Sir Jack Hayward to the players, some of them household names, some scarcely heard of outside the Midlands, but who have all given me – and thousands of other fans to whom Wolves have been an integral part of our lives in good times and ill – a great deal of pleasure.

Geoff Allman
June 2002

Programme for the Wolves *v.* Honved match.

One

The Early Years

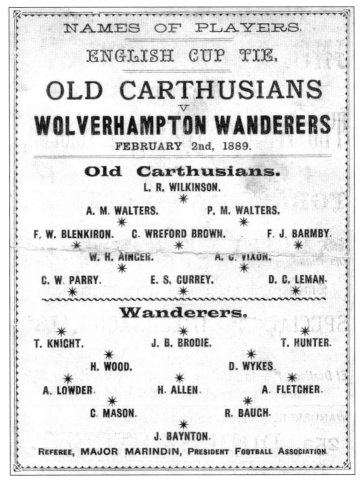

NAMES OF PLAYERS.

ENGLISH CUP TIE.

OLD CARTHUSIANS
v
WOLVERHAMPTON WANDERERS
FEBRUARY 2nd, 1889.

Old Carthusians.
L. R. WILKINSON.
*

A. M. WALTERS.   P. M. WALTERS.
*   *

F. W. BLENKIRON.   C. WREFORD BROWN.   F. J. BARMBY.
*   *   *

W. H. AINGER.   A. C. VIXON.
*   *

C. W. PARRY.   E. S. CURREY.   D. C. LEMAN.
*   *   *

Wanderers.
*   *   *
T. KNIGHT.   J. B. BRODIE.   T. HUNTER.
*   *
H. WOOD.   D. WYKES.
*   *   *
A. LOWDER.   H. ALLEN.   A. FLETCHER.
*   *
C. MASON.   R. BAUGH.
*
J. BAYNTON.

REFEREE, MAJOR MARINDIN, PRESIDENT FOOTBALL ASSOCIATION.

This match card is believed to be the earliest known Wolves programme. It is interesting to note that the referee was the distinguished president of the Football Association Major Marindin, who also refereed several of the early FA Cup finals (or the English Cup, as it was commonly referred to at that time). This game at Dudley Road was a first round tie and seems to have been something of a humdinger, with Wolves coming out winners 4-3 with goals by Tom Knight (2), Charlie Mason and David Wykes. Charlie was capped 3 times by England, while David died tragically young at the age of twenty-eight in 1895, just twenty-four hours after playing in his 179th game for Wolves.

FOOTBALL.

(The letter L indicates a League match.)

WOLVERHAMPTON WANDERERS V. ASTON VILLA (L).

A large assemblage of spectators congregated in the Dudley Road ground, Wolverhampton, on Saturday, to witness the first of the League matches which has been played in the Black Country district. The competing teams were the Wolverhampton Wanderers and the Aston Villa, and much interest was evinced in the match, as both teams had commenced the season victoriously. The clubs, too, are old antagonists, some very severe contests having taken place between them, and inasmuch as the Wanderers' team has been greatly strengthened this season in the forward rank, which has been its weakest point hitherto, there was a general feeling among the followers of the club that the Wolves would defeat the visitors, and much disappointment was shown at the result of the game, the Wanderers, though playing with much determination and vigour, failing on several occasions to take advantage of opportunities which presented themselves for making goals. On the other hand the Villa missed one or two chances. On both sides there were defects noticeable which will no doubt disappear when the men have played together a little oftener. The game throughout was a fast one, and many individual instances of skill and dash were witnessed and evoked much applause. The Villa kicked off up hill, with the wind, and at once assumed the aggressive, Baynton having to kick out. A splendid run on the part of the Wanderers followed, ending in the ball striking the uprights. The visitors, however, succeeded in clearing their lines, and the home goal was next besieged, a corner proving fruitless. Getting hold of the ball again, the Wolves' forward division made a neat run, and the ball was shot over the cross-bar. Both sides played pluckily and with much determination, the back division in each instance, however, being too strong to enable the ball to be driven through successfully. After nearly half an hour's play, however, the Wanderers got the ball down the field, and being centred to White, that player headed it through amid cheers. This reverse put the Villa on their mettle, and they rushed the ball uphill, and it struck the upright and bounded through, the goalkeeper failing to save an easy and flukey shot. At half-time the score stood one goal each. On resuming each side secured a free kick close to goal, but without result. Some very fine runs were executed, but the back divisions proved themselves to be too strong, though the Wanderers early struck the crossbar, and later on a fine opening presented itself, but the ball was kicked right into the goalkeeper's hands, though there was plenty of room to have shot it through. Neither side succeeded in altering the score, and the match ended in a draw of one goal each. Teams:—*Aston Villa:* Warner, goal; Cox and Coulton, backs; Yates, Devey, and Dawson, half-backs; Brown and Green (right), Allen (centre), Garvey and Hodgetts (left) forwards.—*Wanderers:* Baynton, goal; Mason and Baugh, backs; Fletcher, Allen, and Lowder, half-backs; White and Cannon (left), Anderson (centre), Cooper and Hunter (right) forwards. Referee, Mr. Chaplin.

It is interesting to note that in this match report of Wolves' first-ever Football League game, the area in which they played is already being referred to as the 'Black Country'. It is also interesting that although this report was published in a Birmingham newspaper, Villa's goal was attributed to goalkeeper John Baynton's failure to save 'an easy and flukey shot'. John was then in the last of his twelve seasons with Wolves, in the course of which he played in a number of outfield positions before settling in goal towards the end of his career.

Wolves' first major trophy was the 'Challenge Cup of the Football Association' as the FA Cup was then known. The game was played at Fallowfield, Manchester and as a momento of this great win, a row of houses in Dudley Road, Wolverhampton was named 'Fallowfield Terrace'.

WOLVERHAMPTON WANDERERS V. EVERTON.

Although a weekly newspaper has little scope for dealing with football – the evening papers having the advantage in this respect—there are special reasons why the important English Cup final, between the Wolverhampton Wanderers and Everton should be dealt with in the columns of a Walsall newspaper. Not only does Walsall find a strong representation in the conquering team, but the manner in which the Wolverhampton Wanderers, left early in the competition as "the sole hope of the Midlands," fought onward to the very goal of their ambition, deserves all the praise that can be bestowed upon them.

Looking at the names, the three true and tried Walsall players – Allen, Wood, and Wykes —do honour to this town, more especially because one of these scored the only goal, and consequently the winning goal of the match. This goal was at first put down to Wykes, but later reports speak of Allen as the scorer of the all important "unit" which won for the "Wolves," for the first time, the greatest of all football honours. The evening papers not only published the portraits of the players, but gave to each player a history of considerable length, dating from his earliest movements. Not only do Wood, Wykes, and Allen hail from Walsall, but this is the town also where Griffin "first saw the light," for it is recorded for the information of "all and sundry" that he was born here. No less than six of the men were born within seven miles of the Wolverhampton ground.

The match which took place at the Manchester Athletic ground, at Fallowfield, attracted the largest gate ever known, a gate computed at 50,000 spectators, the proceeds amounting to no less a sum than £2,500.

Particulars of the game have been already given at great length. The game in the first half was evenly fought and there was no advantage in the way of scoring. But in the second half Harry Allen put a long shot, and Butcher tackling the Everton goalkeeper, the latter was unable to stop the ball from passing into the net. There was at once tumultous cheering.

The scene, at Wolverhampton, when the result was finally declared almost passes comprehension. As stated by the Press "Wolverhampton went mad with joy. Long before the time announced for the return of the team, the roads to the great Western Station were blocked with people, fog signals were placed all along the line to announce the arrival of the train, blue fires were lighted, and the station seemed enveloped in a blaze of blue flame."

Sir Alfred Hickman carried the Cup, and holding it aloft exclaimed "We have won the English Cup. It has been won by an English team in an honest straightforward English manner." The uproarious cheering testified to the truthfulness of the statement.

CUSTODIAN.

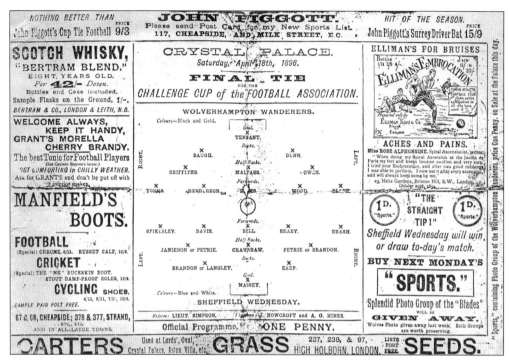

Wolves were in the final again in 1896, but this time they went down 2-1 to Sheffield Wednesday in what was described in a contemporary report as 'a rattling good game'. Wolves were commended for their late rally, that almost brought an equaliser, and a report of the time read 'The efforts of the Wanderers to snatch the result out of the fire will not soon be forgotten by those who were fortunate enough to be present'. This was the second final to be played at Crystal Palace, and it is interesting to note that of the attendance of 58,000, it was reckoned that 48,856 paid for admission, 7,000 were season ticket holders and in addition 'there was a small army of press representatives besides a number to whom complimentary briefs were issued'.

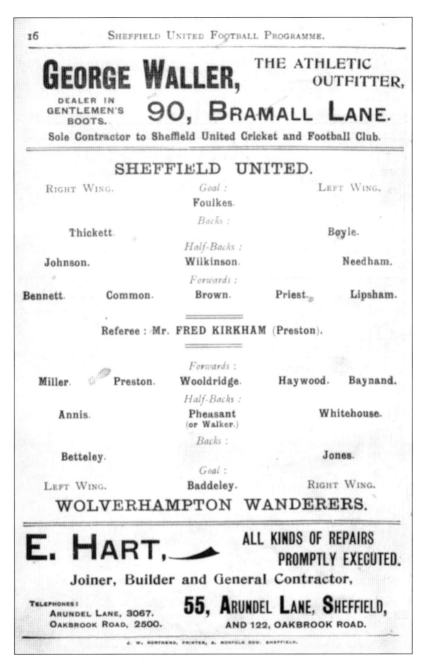
Wolves held their place in the First Division of the Football League for the first eighteen seasons of its existence, but they did suffer some heavy defeats in between times. One of them was in this game at Sheffield United's Bramall Lane, when they went down 7-2 on 17 October 1901. Two quite remarkable goalkeepers played in this game, with Billy Foulke (who weighed over twenty stones) between the sticks for United and Tom Baddeley minding the Wolves net – albeit on this occasion none too successfully. Billy went on to win an England cap four years later, while Tom, despite standing at only 5ft 9in, played 315 games for Wolves between 1897 and 1907 and won 5 England caps.

J.WHITEHOUSE, J.JONES. R.BETTELEY. G.WALKER, T.BADDELEY. W.ANNIS.
A.BAYNAM. A.HAYWOOD. W.WOOLDRIDGE. J.SMITH. J.MILLER.

Wolves finally lost their First Division place in 1906, despite winning their last two games in style (6-1 against Notts County and 7-0 against Derby County). The playing staff was restructured to such an extent that of the line-up for their penultimate season in the First Division in 1904/05, the only survivor to the second season in the Second Division in 1907/08 was defender Billy Wooldridge, who scored 90 goals in 356 games for Wolves between 1900 and 1911.

WOLVERHAMPTON WANDERERS

JONES
LUNN
COLLINS
KENNETH HUNT
WOOLDRIDGE
BISHOP
HARRISON
HEDLEY
PEDLEY
SHELTON
RADFORD

The English Cup Team, 1908

Copyright.

Second Division football did not prevent Wolves from winning the FA Cup in 1908. They beat Newcastle, who had won the trophy in 1906 and the Football League in 1907, 3-1 with the decisive goal coming from Bill Harrison, whose wife had given birth to triplets earlier the same day. By this time Billy Wooldridge, who had for so many seasons been banging home the goals up front, was playing a more defensive role and another key figure in the team was clergyman Revd K.R.G. Hunt, who played as an amateur but still won 2 full England caps after moving from Wolves to Leyton.

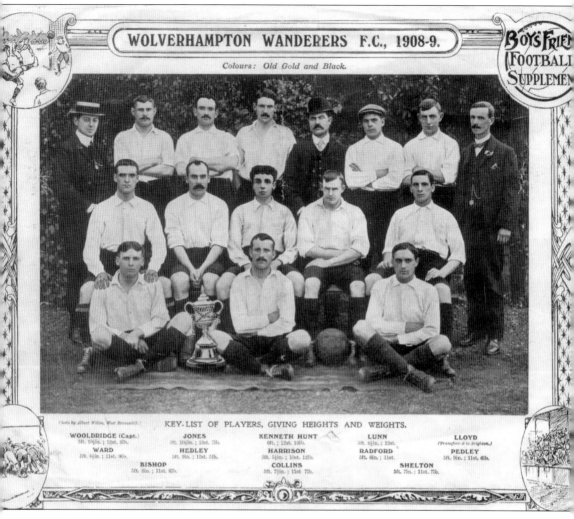

WOLVERHAMPTON WANDERERS F.C., 1908-9.

Colours: Old Gold and Black.

Photo by Albert Wilkes, West Bromwich.

KEY-LIST OF PLAYERS, GIVING HEIGHTS AND WEIGHTS.

WOOLDRIDGE (Capt.)	JONES	KENNETH HUNT	LUNN	LLOYD
5ft. 10½in. ; 12st. 8lb.	5ft. 10½in. ; 13st. 7lb.	6ft. ; 12st. 10lb.	5ft. 8½in. ; 12st.	*(Transferred to Brighton.)*
WARD	HEDLEY	HARRISON	RADFORD	PEDLEY
5ft. 8½in. ; 11st. 9lb.	5ft. 9in. ; 12st. 6lb.	5ft. 5½in. ; 10st. 12lb.	5ft. 8in. ; 11st.	5ft. 9in. ; 11st. 6lb.
	BISHOP	COLLINS	SHELTON	
	5ft. 8in. ; 11st. 8lb.	5ft. 7½in. ; 11st. 7lb.	5ft. 7in. ; 11st. 7lb.	

Wolves kicked off the 1908/09 season as English Cup holders and they had high hopes of a promotion bid, but the new campaign was something of an anti-climax as they finished in seventh place. They would have finished considerably lower but for the sharp-shooting of Walter Radford, who in his second spell with the club banged home 21 of the 56 goals scored by the team.

Wolves' secretary-manager Jack Addenbrook (in the trilby hat in the middle of the line-up) was awarded a long-service medal by the Football League in 1909 in recognition of his twenty-one years' service, which stretched back to the foundation of the Football League in 1888. He remained in this office until the summer of 1922.

Wolves' gates in that 1908/09 season averaged just 8,620, at a time when the best-supported Second Division side were Tottenham Hotspur (with an average of 20,255). At the other end of the spectrum, Glossop's average gates were just 3,430 and the side dropped into the Lancashire Combination in 1915. Another of Wolves' Second Division opponents in tha 1908/09 season were Gainsborough Trinity, whose average gates were 5,380 and who dropped into the Midland League in 1912.

Wolves lost at both Glossop and Gainsborough in that 1908/09 season, but they did gain one of only four away wins in the local derby at West Bromwich when 28,600 saw them win 2-0.

1910/11 was another rather ordinary season for Wolves as far as results were concerned, as they finished in ninth position in the Second Division, although two most interesting players are to be found in the second row of this photograph, which shows the 1910/11 team. Jack Needham (middle of second row) had just arrived from Birmingham and one of the players who had just moved on to make room for him in Wolves' front line was Jack Shelton, who had gone to Port Vale. Little did anyone realise at the time that Jack Shelton would die at a relatively young age and that his widow would in due course marry Jack Needham. What's more, Jack Shelton's son (also named Jack) also played for Wolves in wartime games – this meant that the original Mrs Shelton had two husbands and a son all of whom played for Wolves. Sitting on Jack Needham's right in this group is Albert Groves, who played for Aberdare before coming to Wolves in 1909 and, despite his small stature (he stood 5ft 7in tall), played in 217 games as a defensive midfielder and later gave good service to Walsall.

Fans do seem to have had their request for a more 'go ahead policy' answered, as amongst the new players obtained for 1911/12 was Irish international Billy Halligan from Derby County. He got 24 goals in 39 games in his first season, including a hat-trick in a 8-0 win over hitherto unbeaten Hull in November. This still stands as Hull's heaviest ever defeat in the Football League.

DISSATISFACTION AT WOLVERHAMPTON.

Considerable dissatisfaction prevails in Wolverhampton at the position of the Wanderers, and many supporters of the club are advocating a more go-ahead policy. At present it is impossible to ascertain what new players have been signed on, but three at least have been secured.

Speaking at a Wolverhampton gathering on Friday, Mr. Charles Crump (senior vice-president of the F.A.) said they wanted senior football in the town to have more life in it. If the club aimed high the local public would be as keen in their appreciation and support as they had been in the past.

HACKNEY EMPIRE

6.45.   **TWICE NIGHTLY.**   **9 P.M.**

ENGLISH LEAGUE.

CLAPTON ORIENT v. WOLVERHAMPTON W.

CLAPTON ORIENT.

Colours—WHITE SHIRTS, BLUE KNICKERS.

Goal.
1 HUGALL.

Backs.
2 HIND.   3 EVANS.

Half-backs.
4 FORREST.   5 SCOTT.   6 GIBSON.

Forwards.

Right Wing.		Centre.		Left Wing.
PARKER.	DALRYMPLE.	JONAS.	McFADDEN.	DIX.
7	8	9	10	11

Referee — Mr. A. PELLOWE.

Forwards.

Left Wing.		Centre.		Right Wing
BROOKS.	NEEDHAM.	CURTIS.	LANGFORD.	HARRISON.
12	13	14	15	16

Half-backs.
17 BISHOP.   18 GROVES.   19 PRICE.

Backs.
20 COLLINS.   21 GARRATLY.

Goal.
22 PEERS.

WOLVERHAMPTON WANDERERS.

Colours—OLD GOLD AND BLACK STRIPES.

Linesmen—Messrs. A. GODDARD & E. M. MITTON

Though the First World War had begun, League football continued as best it could for the whole of the 1914/15 season and Clapton Orient (the former name of Leyton Orient) were one of the clubs to continue to produce an eight-page programme. This was the opening game of the new season against Wolves and it ended 1-1, with Alf Bishop, Ted Collins and Bill Harrison surviving from the 1908 FA Cup win. By that time Teddy Peers, another relatively diminutive player, had taken over in goal and had already won the first of his 14 Welsh international caps.

Sammy Brooks was one of the players whose careers for Wolves bridged the First World War. Playing on the left flank of the attack, he made his debut in April 1911 and was still in the Wolves side that reached the final of the FA Cup in 1921, totalling 246 games and scoring 53 goals – not for nothing was Sammy known as the 'Little Giant'.

TEAMS FOR TO-DAY'S MATCH—SATURDAY, APRIL 10th, 1915.

BIRMINGHAM LEAGUE CHAMPIONSHIP.
(Match No. 33.)

Wolverhampton Wanderers Reserves v. Aston Villa Reserves.

Kick-off at 3.30 p.m.

WOLVERHAMPTON WANDERERS RESERVES.

Right.   Left.

W. HAYES (1)

BROOKS (2)   PARFITT (3)

SMART (4)   RILEY (5)   BROOKES (6)

J. W. HAYES (7)   DUNN (8)   GRIFFITHS (9)   RICHARDS (10)   LEA (11)

Referee : MR. J. MASON (Burslem).

KILNER (12)   A. H. CROSS (13)   BOYNE (14)   W. H. WALKER (15)   E. O. WOOD (16)

WHITTAKER (17)   MOSS (18)   H. J. HOOTON (19)

GRIFFITHS (20)   TRANTER (21)

Left.   ANSTEY (22)   Right.

ASTON VILLA RESERVES.

In the event of any alteration in the above teams, a board giving particulars will be sent round the ground.

This was one of the last games played by a Wolves team before the club closed down until the end of hostilities. Aston Villa were then in the First Division and Wolves in the second, so the Midland neighbours did not meet at first-team level, but both teams' reserves were in the Birmingham League. In the Wolves side on this particular day were Alf Riley and Tansy Lea, both of whom were destined to play in the 1921 FA Cup final, while the Villa team contained the legendary Billy Walker from Hednesford, who went on to win 18 England caps between the wars and managed Nottingham Forest after the Second World War.

Two
Between the Wars

Wolves had finished in their lowest-ever League position in the first season after the First World War, ending up in nineteenth spot in 1919/20. However, hopes were raised for the 1920/21 season with the signing of George Edmonds from Watford. He was the top scorer with 15 League and cup goals in that first season and went on to score 42 goals in 136 games. On one memorable occasion, a shot of his actually burst the net – and the goal was disallowed. George is thought to have been the longest living of all Wolves players, as he reached the age of ninety-six before his death in December 1989.

Wolves first issued an eight-page match programme (as opposed to the pre-First World War single-page cards) in 1920. This was the second season after the First World War, and their opponents included South Shields, who had only come into the Football League the season before. This North Eastern club changed their name to Gateshead in 1930 and dropped out of the Football League altogether in 1960 when replaced by Peterborough. Wolves won this particular game 3-0, with George Edmonds, Sammy Brooks and Fred Burrill on the mark in front of just 7,443 fans on a cold December day.

The Wolverhampton Wanderers
Official Programme & Club's Record.

No. 17, Vol. 1.　　　December 11, 1920.　　　Twopence.

Wolverhampton Wanderers F.C.

Registered Office :—
Molineux Grounds, Wolverhampton.
TELEPHONE : No. 1197.

The Wolverhampton Wanderers
Official Programme & Club's Record.
DECEMBER 11, 1920.

Wolves' News.

A BRIGHTER OUTLOOK.
By "Black and Gold."

DAME FORTUNE has, at last, considered it prudent to smile on the Wolves, who have more than justified the confidence reposed in them by their more ardent supporters in securing a handsome victory by the odd goal in three. There were those who considered the Wolves had shot their bolt, but although such thoughts were always looming largely,

there was always a something which kept saying that the Wolves were a clever set and must sooner or later display form calculated to shock football enthusiasts throughout the country. We received the shock on Saturday, but it was an extremely pleasant one for all of us, many of whom were of opinion that it was impossible for the team to capture the full complement from a team who had made the running in the league since the commencement of the season.

I, personally, never entertained any doubts as to the ability of the players to give a perfect exposition of the true art of football, but this could not be done successfully until they received encouragement and a fair distribution of "luck." The success last week-end was thoroughly deserved, for in every department there was cohesion and an abandon about all the movements, which spell success. All the forwards seem to revel in the mud, and as I ventured to prophesy that the pivot would come into his own as soon as the ground began to be heavy has proved correct. A more judicious and tenacious centre-forward no one could have wished to see : he led the quintette with tact and ability, and it was surprising that South Shields were not humiliated to a greater extent.

It would be unfair to individualise, for everyone played a great game considering the unenviable conditions, which could not have been worse.

The Directors must be congratulated on their business acumen, together, of course, with their enterprise, which has proved so very lucrative so far. Those who have been disappointed in the past will, I venture to suggest, find great satisfaction in the displays of the future, which look extremely bright ; in fact, the outlook has never been brighter, at least since the Armistice. There has been a general tightening up all round, and with an efficient trainer there is no reason why we should not attain to great heights.

The form of the Reserves fluctuates considerably, and when everyone expects a decisive win the reverse actually happens. Under such weather conditions experienced at Molineux, no one could have been surprised at anything happening, but it must be said that Wellington thoroughly deserved their victory. They possess an extremely clever side, and they are to be congratulated on their smart victory.

The Publisher will be pleased to consider any letters or communications of interest.

All communications to be addressed to—
A. H. PAULTON, Berry Street, Wolverhampton.

TEAMS FOR TO-DAY'S MATCH.

League Championship.—Match No. 18.

South Shields v. Wolves.

Colours : Green and Red Shirts,　　Colours : Old Gold & Black Shirts,
White Knickers.　　　　　　　　　Black Knickers.

Referee—Mr. J. H. ALDERSON, Earlestown.　Linesmen—A. TIMMINS & F. EDWARDS

SOUTH SHIELDS.

Right.　　　　　　　　　　　　　　　Left

WALKER (1)

CRESSWELL (2)　　　　　MAITLAND (3)

DREYER (4)　　HOPKINS (5)　　HAMPSON (6)

KEENLYSIDE (7)　WOODS (8)　LILLYCROP (9)　HAWES (10)　PARKER (11)

BROOKS (12)　POTTS (13)　EDMONDS (14)　BURRILL (15)　BRICE (16)

RILEY (17)　　HODNETT (18)　　GREGORY (19)

MARSHALL (20)　　　　BAUGH (21)

PEERS (22)

Left.　　　　　　　　　　　　　　Right.

WOLVES.

In the event of any alteration in the above teams, the same will appear in the frame above the Result Board.

To-day's Half-time and Full-time Scores as shown on Board.

Letter	MATCH.	Half-time	Final.	Letter	MATCH.	Half-time	Final.	Letter	MATCH.	Half-time	Final.
A	Arsenal / Chelsea			J	Sheffield U. / Tottenham			S	Port Vale / Stockport		
B	Aston Villa / Newcastle			K	Sunderland / W. B. Albion			T	Rotherham / Bury		
C	Bolton / Huddersfield			L	Burnley / Bristol			U	West Ham / Stoke		
D	Bradford / Manchester U.			M	Cardiff / Sheffield W.			V	Wellington / Wolves Res.		
E	Burnley / Liverpool			N	Coventry / Birmingham			W	Brentford / Luton		
F	Derby / Blackburn			O	Fulham / Clapton			X	Bristol Rovers / Reading		
G	Middlesbrough			P	Leeds / Notts County			Y	Crystal Palace / Swansea		
H	Manchester C. / Bradford C.			Q	Leicester / Blackpool			Z	Grimsby Town / Southampton		
I	Preston N. E. / Oldham			R	Notts Forest / Hull City						

NOTE :—The Spectators will decipher the Board by taking the First Club and Figure as the Home Club and Score.

Wolves again belied their Second Division status by reaching the final of the FA Cup in 1921. They were in mid-table when they took on Spurs, who were lying sixth in the First Division, at Stamford Bridge and only a cross-shot from Spurs winger Jimmy Dimmock separated the clubs as the game ended 1-0.

SPURS BEAT WOLVES IN THE FINAL.

Stubborn Struggle in the Mud at Stamford Bridge.

Tottenham Hotspur and Wolverhampton Wanderers met at Stamford Bridge this afternoon in the final of the English Cup contest.

The ground was packed long before the kick-off, and thousands left outside clamoured for admission.

The King was present, and shook hands with the players after they had entered the field.

After a stubbornly-contested game in the mud, Tottenham ran out winners by one goal to nothing. The Wolves were beaten, but certainly not disgraced.

Following a goalless first half Dimmock scored for the 'Spurs nine minutes after the resumption, amidst scenes of tremendous enthusiasm.

It is interesting to note that this young player, who this year received international honours, was just born when Tottenham won the Cup twenty years ago.

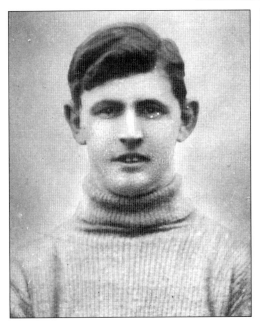

Two of Wolves' FA Cup final stalwarts were Noel George (*above left*) and Fred Burrill (*above right*). Noel, who had been a forward with Hednesford before the war, became a goalkeeper while serving with the RASC in Salonika during hostilities and the FA Cup final was only his fourteenth first-team appearance. Sadly, after 242 first-team games, Noel was cruelly struck down with a terminal illness and he died in 1929 aged just thirty-two. Fred had played in the Southern League with both West Ham and Southend before the First World War and was a typical inside forward of his day – a schemer who could score goals. Like many other Wolves players over the years, he later played for Walsall in the Third Division.

Many Wolves fans thought the end of the world had come when, just two years after being watched by a 72,805 gate in the FA Cup final at Stamford Bridge, they were relegated to the Third Division (North) and found themselves playing in front of just 6,500 in an early-season game at Crewe. Happily, this relegation proved to be a blessing in disguise as, under manager George Jobey (a Newcastle United First Division championship winner in his playing days), Wolves roared to instant promotion as they lost only three League games all season and scored 76 goals against 27.

One of Wolves' most spectacular wins in that promotion season was by a 7-1 margin at luckless Ashington in January 1924, against a North Eastern team who survived in the Third Division (North) from 1921 to 1929, when they were succeeded by York City. Ashington are still very much alive, however, playing in Division One of the Northern League in 2001/02. Two of the goals at Ashington were scored by Stan Fazackerley (left). Stan was signed from Everton in November 1922 and scored 32 goals in 77 games for Wolves. He subsequently played for Derby County for a short spell.

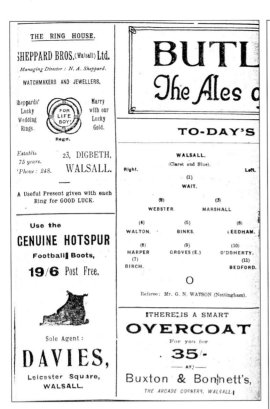
One of Wolves' three defeats during that promotion season was at lowly neighbours Walsall, who on a Monday evening in April beat them 2-1 in front of a 12,281 gate (although a number of other people watched the game for free after a gate had given way under the pressure of the crowd outside).

Our Visitors.

WOLVERHAMPTON WANDERERS.

IT is as the prospective champions of the Northern Section that Wolverhampton Wanderers come to Hillary Street to-day, but they are not yet assured of the honour, and therefore they may be depended on to go " all out " for the two points which will still further improve their prospects of securing their " return ticket " to the Second Division. A great deal of water has flown under the bridges since last the Wanderers' first team visited Walsall, for when we were in the Second Division they were in the First. Assuming that they gain promotion this season, how long will it be, we wonder, before we meet them again? Not being gifted with the prophetic instinct, we cannot pretend to answer the question.

One interesting feature about the Wanderers' side is that it possesses a strong local element. Noel George, the goalkeeper, for instance, hails from Lichfield; H. Shaw, the left full-back, from Hednesford; W. Caddick, the centre-half, from Wolverhampton; and J. Harrington, the outside-right, from Brownhills; whilst Geo. Getgood, although Glasgow born, has lived in the district for a long time. They have also on their list other products of Midland football in R. Baugh, R. Spencer and E. Legge, of Wolverhampton; F. Marson, of Darlaston; A. Picken, of Wellington; C. Price and F. Pickering, of St. George's; and, of course, B. Timmins and T. Bowen, whom we recently transferred to them.

E. Watson, the right back, owns Newcastle as his birthplace, and T. R. Davison, centre-half, comes from West Stanley, which is in the same part of the country. Of the forwards, J. Lees is a native of Nottingham, E. Edwards, the outside-right, belongs to Glamorgan, and Martin, the centre-forward, joined them from Aberdare, after having previously been with Stoke. Phillipson, another centre-forward on their books, was obtained from Swindon about three months ago.

Last, but by no means least, there is Stanley Fazackerley, the inside-right, who has rendered the Wanderers such yeoman service since they secured his transfer from Everton. A native of Preston, Fazackerley has worn the colours of the famous North End and Hull, but it was whilst with Sheffield United that he achieved most distinction, including selection as a member of the English team which visited South Africa in 1920. Apparently he took his shooting boots with him, too, for his " bag " for the tour was 18 goals. In the same year also, he played for the North v. England in the trial match at Newcastle.

One of Wolves' greatest-ever strikers was Tommy Phillipson, who was signed from Swindon in December 1923. By the time he had moved to Sheffield United in February 1928, he had scored 111 goals in 159 games. He later played for Walsall and in 1938 he was elected mayor of Wolverhampton. After the Second World War, he was for many years a newsagent in Darlington Street, Wolverhampton.

Even more significant than the signing of Tommy Phillipson in 1923 was the acquisition of Major Frank Buckley as manager in 1927. This remarkable man had served in both the Boer War and the First World War, and played in the Aston Villa defence in between. He managed both Blackpool and Norwich before coming to Wolves, whom he transformed from a Second Division outfit to one of the country's top First Division teams, paying particular attention to the development of homegrown talent.

An illustration taken from the special souvenir brochure that was published at the time: these are the men who helped Wolves back to the top flight in 1932 after an absence of twenty-six years.

Leading scorer in Wolves' promotion season was Billy Hartill, who proved a more-than-adequate successor to Tommy Phillipson when signed by Wolves in 1928 after his demobilisation from the army. Known as 'Hartillery', Bill's 170 goals in 234 games for Wolves included 30 in the promotion season.

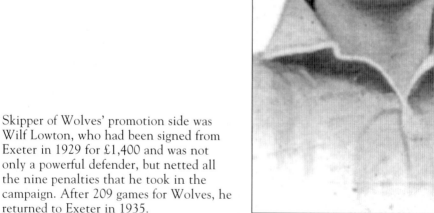

Skipper of Wolves' promotion side was Wilf Lowton, who had been signed from Exeter in 1929 for £1,400 and was not only a powerful defender, but netted all the nine penalties that he took in the campaign. After 209 games for Wolves, he returned to Exeter in 1935.

One of the features of football up to the 1960s was that League teams usually played at least one pre-season public practice match. In Wolves' case, the two sides were consistently known as 'Colours' (wearing gold shirts) and 'Whites' (wearing white shirts). The line-ups in these 1935 games indicate just how Major Buckley relied on homegrown talent – none of the players involved in the practice games cost above £1,000 and yet all except outside left Miller played in Wolves' first team at one time or other.

The goalkeeper in the 'Whites' side was Jimmy Utterson, who died in December 1935 after receiving a serious head injury in a game at Middlesbrough. The 'Club Notes' in the programme read: 'The tragic death of James Utterson at mid-day on the Friday before the Stoke match cast a gloom over Molineux Grounds, and it was a hushed and sorrowing party that travelled in the charabanc to the Potteries on Saturday last. The loss of such a bright personality and comrade reacted very severely on some of the younger boys and everyone sympathised with his bed-mate, Joe Gardiner ... Utterson will be greatly missed, always bright and cheery he was the "crooner" of the Club and until this last few weeks was irrepressible. That he had suffered uncomplainingly for some time is now quite apparent and his death is a shock to us all.'

Prices of Admission and Entrances:

GROUND:	1st team	Res. team	ENTRANCE
Hotel End	1/-	6d.	Molineux Hotel
			Molineux Alley
			Doors A & B, Molineux St.
			Door B, Waterloo Road
Bushbury End	1/-	6d.	Door J, Waterloo Road
			Door N, Molineux Street
Hotel End (Boys)	6d.	5d.	{ Door B, Molineux Street
			{ Molineux Hotel
Bushbury End (Boys)	6d.	5d.	Door N, Molineux Street

WATERLOO ROAD STAND:

	1st team	Res. team	ENTRANCE
Centre	3/-	2/-	Door G, Waterloo Road
Centre (Boys)	1/6	1/-	Door G, Waterloo Road
Hotel Wing & Enclosure	2/-	1/6	Door D, Waterloo Road
Bushbury Wing	2/-	1/6	Door H, Waterloo Road
Wing Stand (Boys)	1/-	9d.	Door E, Waterloo Road

MOLINEUX STREET STAND:

	1st team	Res. team	ENTRANCE
Centre	2/6	1/-	Doors F & G, Molineux St.
Centre (Boys)	1/3	6d.	Door H, Molineux Street
Hotel Wing	2/-	1/-	Doors D & E, Molineux St.
Hotel Wing (Boys)	1/-	6d.	*Door E, Molineux Street
Bushbury Wing	2/-	1/-	Door J, Molineux Street
Enclosure	1/6	1/-	Doors I & M, Molineux St.
Enclosure (Boys)	9d.	6d.	Door M, Molineux Street

* Only Entrance at Reserve Matches for Molineux St. Stand (All Parts)

SEASON TICKETS ARE NOW ON SALE:

Waterloo Rd. Stand (Centre) Numbered and Reserved Seat	£3/7/6
Waterloo Rd. Stand (Wings) Numbered and Reserved Seat	£2/15/0
Molineux St. Stand (Centre) Numbered and Reserved Seat	£2/15/0
Molineux St. Stand (Wings) Unreserved }	£2/5/0
Waterloo Rd. Stand (Wings) Unreserved }	£2/5/0
Ground (both ends)	£1/5/0

All of the above prices include Entertainment Tax.

A few mouths may water at this list of admission prices in 1935. As will be seen the top price for a season ticket was £3/7/6 – only just over a pound more than a single match programme today. It really did seem value for money as Wolves kicked off with a 3-2 win over Birmingham, for whom Harry Hibbs (the current England goalkeeper) was in goal. Irish international winger Jackie Brown got two of Wolves' goals – after three season with Wolves, he moved on to the Blues in 1938.

1871 — MOLINEUX GROUNDS — 1935

The match programme also published pictures that compared the way Molineux had developed from a park in 1871 to an impressive ground in 1935. The latter picture is taken from the hotel end, with the Waterloo Road stand on the left, the 'Cowshed' at the Bushbury end straight in front and the Molineux Street stand on the right.

In 1871 the excellent gardens incorporated a boating lake, a band stand and an athletics and cycle track which surrounded the sporting field. Wolves actually played a Walsall Cup semi-final there in 1886 against Walsall Town. This was three years before Wolves made their new home there, and it was in September 1889 that they played their first League game there against Notts County – and won 2-0. They had played at the Dudley Road ground in their first Football League season in 1888/89.

FOUR GOALS IN LAST TEN MINUTES

"Doubles" for Wrigglesworth and Phillips

ROVERS GET FIRST BITE, AND THEN—

(By Nomad)

Wolves made a meal of Blackburn Rovers at Molineux this afternoon. Rovers got the first "bite," but afterwards the visitors were torn to pieces, Wolves winning by 8—1.

IT was Wolves' biggest win since they beat Manchester City 8—0 at Molineux on December 23rd, 1933. That season, incidentally, Wolves lost 7—1 at Blackburn. There's nothing like going one better !

GOAL LOG AT MOLINEUX		
Halsall (Blackburn)...	4	min.
Jones	10	"
Thompson	3½	"
Wrigglesworth	44	"
Gardiner	62	"
Phillips	80	"
Phillips	82	"
Wrigglesworth	88	"
Crook (own goal)	89	"

front of Wolves goal and dribbled up t

One of the characteristics of sides put together by Major Buckley was that they usually scored goals and often lasted the pace better than opponents – as was the case in this game against Blackburn in November 1935, when four of the eight goals came in the last ten minutes. It was significant, however, that a disproportionate number of Wolves' goals were scored at home. In 1935/36 they netted 59 goals at Molineux and just 18 on their travels.

Charlie Phillips joined Wolves from Ebbw Vale in 1929. He was the flying winger who got 2 goals in the space of 3 minutes in the runaway victory over Blackburn described in the article above. He got 19 goals in the 1931/32 promotion season and went on to total 65 goals in 202 games before moving to Aston Villa in 1936. He also won 10 Welsh caps and captained his country on six occasions.

This sheet of reserve-team autographs from the mid-1930s includes winger Billy Barraclough, who had been in the 1931/32 promotion side, and goalkeeper Cyril Spiers – who was one of the few players to be bought by Major Buckley from another League club (Spurs) and who went on to manage Norwich after the Second World War. Right at the bottom is Joe Gardiner, the midfielder who made his first-team debut in 1935 and was first-team trainer during the glory years of the 1950s.

One of Wolves' greatest-ever defenders, Stan Cullis made his first-team debut against Huddersfield in February 1935. He was appointed captain in the following season at the age of twenty and went on to play 171 first-team games plus 31 wartime games, as well as winning 12 England caps. Yet Stan was to become even more famous as Wolves' manager, leading them to three League Championships in the 1950s and FA Cup wins in 1949 and 1960.

When Stan Cullis made his League debut, Mark Crook had just played the last of his 81 games on Wolves' right or left wing. Mark, who stood just 5ft 5in, then moved to Luton, but he too had still to make his greatest contribution to Wolves' success as, during the war, he formed a Yorkshire club known as Wath Wanderers, from where he sent a wealth of talent to Molineux – his protégés including England men Ron Flowers, Eddie Clamp and Alan Sunderland.

A fellow defender in Stan's debut game was Reg Hollingworth, who joined Wolves from Sutton Junction FC in November 1928 and went straight into the first team, although he was only 19. He was in the promotion team of 1931/32 and had the bad luck to be injured just before he was due to play in an England international trial. He was only twenty-six when injury ended his career in 1935, and there was a final tragedy in his life when he died at the wheel of his car in 1969 aged fifty-nine.

Wolves' Biggest League Win

FOUR EACH FOR DORSETT AND WESTCOTT

By Nomad

MAKING one of the most amazing returns to form imaginable, Wolves swept Leicester City off their legs and created history when they won 10—1 at Molineux yesterday.

Not only did Wolves register their biggest victory ever in Division I., but they gave Leicester the soundest thrashing they have ever had in the senior circle.

Even the goal the visitors got was put into the net by a Wolves player—Cullis.

This magnificent victory, coupled with Arsenal's surprising home defeat against Brentford, put Wolves right back into a real challenging position for the championship.

Wolves previous highest scores since they "came back" were eights against Manchester City and Blackburn Rovers.

After Wolves' failures almost week after week in recent matches, who ever thought they were capable of getting ten goals in one game?

But this time they were a vastly-improved side, and range that alongside the fact that the City defence was the most incapable Wolves have met this season, and you have the answer to your question—how did they manage to get ten.

FORWARDS PLAYED TO EACH OTHER

Wolves team spirit and combination, too, was of a higher standard than it has been for many months. There was hardly any selfishness, and each forward played to the other at all times.

One of the most striking things about this match was that Dorsett, playing at outside-left for the first time for Wolves, got a hat trick in the first half and made his own score four later on.

The manner in which he parted with the ball first time and at the right time was commendable, and, what is more, he took his chances.

Westcott's virile leadership, too, was a feature of the game. He always used the ball intelligently, and his eyes were so wide open for chances that he, too, got four goals.

Wright, the newcomer to first-class football, was the only forward who did not score, but he had a splendid first half, pushing some fine balls out to the wing or up the middle.

There were very few individualistic efforts in the Wolves front line. Every goal was the result of good combination and well-placed passing.

Dowen, in the first team defence once again, started shakily because Dewis and Grosvenor interchanged the ball so rapidly that the back was unable to get in a tackle. He quickly settled down, however, and thereafter little danger came from the Leicester right wing.

City actually began quite as well as Wolves, and it was only a great save by Sidlow that prevented them getting level after Westcott had put his side in front. Shortly afterwards Sidlow was injured in coming out to meet Bowers and Liddle, and was in pain for the rest of the match. By half-time Wolves had a commanding lead of 4—0, and when Jones made it five within three minutes of the resumption, Leicester went right to pieces, and it was then just a matter of how many Wolves would get.

The rejoicing was unbounded when Westcott sent the score into double figures in the last minute.

BOWERS HELD BY CULLIS

Leicester had to reshuffle their attack when Liddle received an injury mid-way through the second half, but the match was won long before then. Throughout

THE GOAL SPATE

This is how the goals came:—

13 minutes	....	Westcott
24 "	....	Dorsett
40 "	....	Dorsett
42 "	....	Dorsett
48 "	....	Jones
52 "	....	Westcott
61 "	....	Maguire
81 "	.. Cullis (own goal)	
83 "	....	Dorsett
85 "	....	Westcott
89 "	....	Westcott

the game Bowers, the former England centre-forward, was in Cullis's pocket, and he did no better when he changed places with Dewis.

Wolves were particularly strong in the half-back line, where Galley and Gardiner, besides defending and covering cleverly, opened out attacks time after time. Morris, too, made his work look easy, although Stubbs was a more useful winger than Grosvenor.

Teams:—

WOLVES. — Sidlow; Morris, Dowen; Galley, Cullis, Gardiner; Maguire, Wright, Westcott, Jones, Dorsett.

LEICESTER CITY. — McLaren; Reeday, Jones; Smith, Heywood, Coutts; Grosvenor, Dewis, Bowers, Liddle, Stubbs.

Referee.—C. E. Argent (St. Alban's).

Official gate 24,540.

There was normally a full programme of League football on Good Fridays between the wars and Wolves certainly made the most of it on 15 April 1938, when they romped home 10-1 against Leicester City. Yet just a day later, they were held to a goal-less draw by Preston at Molineux and on the following Monday they were held to a 1-1 draw in the return game at Leicester.

Eight of the goals in that biggest-ever League win over Leicester were scored by Dick Dorsett (5) and Dennis Westcott (3). This was one of Wolves' greatest-ever twin spearheads. Dick *(left)* hailed from Brownhills and scored 35 goals in 51 games up to the Second World War and 37 in 55 wartime games. He joined Aston Villa in 1946 and gave them great service as a midfielder. Dennis *(right)* came from New Brighton to Wolves in 1936 and either side of the Second World War netted 124 goals in 144 games, plus 90 more in 70 wartime games. He moved to Manchester City in 1948 and gave good service to both them and Chesterfield, ending his career with Stafford Rangers before his untimely death, aged just forty-three, in 1960. Another of the goals in that 10-1 hammering of Leicester was scored by Teddy Maguire, a winger who had joined Wolves in 1936. He scored 9 goals in 85 games up to the Second World War and was equally happy on the right or the left flank of an attack. He played a few games for Hartlepool just after the start of the war, and played for Swindon and Halifax after the hostilities.

Brothers Frank and Jack Taylor partnered each other at full-back for Wolves in several games before the Second World War. Frank totalled 54 first-team games and Jack 89. After the war, Frank managed Stoke from 1932 to 1960 and Jack managed QPR from 1952 to 1959 and Leeds from 1959 to 1961.

SATURDAY, JANUARY 1st, 1938
MANCHESTER CITY

1
SWIFT
Goal

2   3
CLARK   **BARKAS**
Right Back   Left Back

4   5   6
M'CULLOUGH   **MARSHALL**   **BRAY**
Right Half-Back   Centre Half-Back   Left Half-Back

7   8   9   10   11
TOSELAND   **HERD**   **TILSON**   **DOHERTY**   **WARDLE**
Outside Right   Inside Right   Centre   Inside Left   Outside Left

Referee: Linesmen:
E. WOOD, Sheffield   *HYDES ORDER PALE ALE*   A. S. BARNES, Blue Stripe

KICK-OFF 2-15 p.m.   J. H. HARGREAVES, Red Stripe

12   13   14   15   16
KIRKHAM   **GALLEY**   **WESTCOTT**   **JONES**   **ASHALL**
Outside Left   Inside Left   Centre   Inside Right   Outside Right

17   18   19
GARDINER   **CULLIS**   **SMALLEY**
Left Half-Back   Centre Half-Back   Right Half-Back

20   21
TAYLOR (J.)   **TAYLOR (F.)**
Left Back   Right Back

22
SCOTT
Goal

WOLVERHAMPTON W.

This game at Manchester City's Maine Road on New Year's Day 1938 sees the Taylor brothers together in Wolves' defence, while the Manchester City side includes Alec Herd (who was destined in 1951 to play in the same Stockport County front line as his son David Herd). Wolves won the game 4-2, with Tommy Galley (2), Bryn Jones and Dennis Westcott on the mark, while Alec Herd and Peter Doherty got the City goals.

Despite his tremendous success as Wolves manager, Major Buckley was not always the most popular man in Wolverhampton. His habit of selling players and building up the club's finances on the assumption that his tremendous scouting network could always replace them generally worked well, but the fans took exception to this when the player was particularly popular. This happened in the case of Bryn Jones, who was a bargain signing from Aberamon in 1933, scored 57 goals in 177 games for Wolves and won 10 Welsh caps by the summer of 1938. Fans were near to rioting when he was sold to Arsenal – albeit for a record fee at that time of £14,500. Maybe Buckley was right, for Bryan never showed his Wolves form for Arsenal and, with his career losing seven years to the war, he scored just 7 goals in 70 games for Arsenal.

Major Buckley was famous for throwing hitherto untried players into the testing arena of first-team football. A typical example was that of Alan Steen, who was just 16 years 9 months when selected to make his debut against Manchester United at Molineux in March 1939. Alan delivered the goods by banging home the third goal in a 3-0 Wolves win and one can still hear the delighted cry 'The kid's scored', from the fans. Yet this was Alan's only League game for Wolves. He survived a spell as a prisoner of war during hostilities, played 27 wartime games for Wolves, and then after the war had useful spells with Luton, Aldershot, Rochdale and Carlisle.

THE LEAGUE—Division I.

HOME		AWAY	
Birmingham..	1	Grimsby.......	1
Bolton Wand.	3	Huddersfield	2
Charlton......	3	Portsmouth..	3
Chelsea........	1	Brentford.....	3
Leeds Utd...	1	Everton........	2
Leicester C..	1	Aston Villa....	1
Liverpool.....	0	Wolves	2
Man. Utd......	1	Derby C.......	1
Middlesbro'..	3	Sunderland ..	0
Preston N. E.	2	The Arsenal..	1
Stoke City....	1	Blackpool.....	1

RECORD UP TO DATE

	Pld	Won	Lost	Drn	For	Agst	Pts
EVERTON	30	20	8	2	59	37	42
WOLVES	30	16	6	8	61	22	40
DERBY COUNTY	31	16	8	7	54	38	39
MIDDLESBRO	31	14	10	7	65	48	35
CHARLTON ATH	30	15	10	5	55	45	35
BOLTON WAN	30	12	9	9	45	43	33
STOKE CITY	31	12	10				
ASTON VILLA	30	13	11	6	53	42	32
THE ARSENAL	30	11	10	9	35	28	31
LIVERPOOL	30	11	11	8	46	48	30
GRIMSBY	30	11	11	8	42	60	30
PRESTON N E	29	10	10	9	41	42	29
MANCHESTER U	30	9	10	11	45	47	29
BRENTFORD	30	11	13	6	44	58	28
SUNDERLAND	29	10	11	8	36	48	28
LEEDS UNITED	29	10	12	7	45	53	27
BLACKPOOL	29	7	12	10	37	52	24
HUDDERSFIELD	30	9	16	5	43	49	23
LEICESTER CITY	30	7	14	9	35	57	23
PORTSMOUTH	29	6	12	11	27	49	23
CHELSEA	28	8	15	5	47	59	21
BIRMINGHAM	30	8	17	5	46	62	21

1938/39 was the season when Wolves seemed destined to become the first team to do the Football League and FA Cup double since Aston Villa in 1897. By 25 February they were just two points behind Everton in the First Division and had reached the last eight of the FA Cup.

Goalkeeper Alec Scott, who was pelted by oranges during Wolves' 2-0 win at Liverpool, was in fact playing against his former club from where he had moved to Burnley in 1933 and to Wolves in 1936. A big man with a safe pair of hands and remarkable agility for a man of his size, he played 129 games for Wolves up to the Second World War and another 82 wartime games before ending his playing career at Crewe and then keeping a general store for many years in Dunstall Road. What a delight it was for Wolves fans when (in days when goalkeepers had ⸱⸱ protection) onrushing forwards ⸱⸱ed to charge Alec before being ⸱⸱ntle' nudge from Alec's broad ⸱ ending up in the net

POST OFFICE TELEGRAM

Prefix. Time handed in. Office of Origin and Service Instructions. Words.

m 95

From + 195 11.30 WOLVERHAMPTON T 18   To

CULLIS CAPTAIN WOLVES FOOTBALL GROUND GRIMSBY =

= WOLVERHAMPTON EXPECTS EVERY MAN THIS DAY TO DO HIS

DUTY = CHARLES MANDER ++

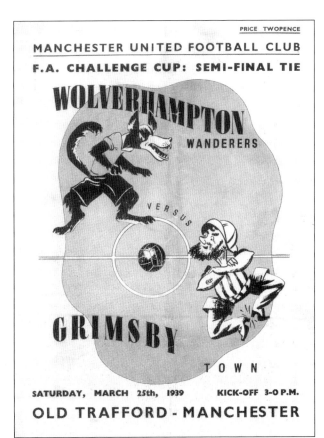

MANCHESTER UNITED FOOTBALL CLUB

PRICE TWOPENCE

F.A. CHALLENGE CUP: SEMI-FINAL TIE

WOLVERHAMPTON WANDERERS

VERSUS

GRIMSBY TOWN

SATURDAY, MARCH 25th, 1939   KICK-OFF 3-0 P.M.

OLD TRAFFORD - MANCHESTER

Though Wolves lost ground in the League battle, they continued to go great guns in the FA Cup with a 2-0 sixth round win over Everton to earn a semi-final tie against Grimsby at Old Trafford. Encouraged by a telegram from their chairman, Sir Charles Mander, and cashing in on an early injury to Grimsby goal-keeper George Moulson (deputising for George Tweedy), Wolves romped home 5-0 with Dickie Dorsett getting four of the goals.

Wolves were the hottest FA Cup favourites for years when they met Portsmouth (seventeenth in the First Division) at Wembley. Looking back, however, one notices that Portsmouth had beaten Wolves at Fratton Park earlier in the season and Wolves had won only four of the nine League games leading up to the final. Be that as it may, the final was very one-sided – and Portsmouth were the only side in it as they romped home 4-1.

To make things worse, one of the Portsmouth goals was scored by Bert Barlow, who had moved to them from Wolves earlier in the season.

Stan 'Dizzy' Burton played on Wolves' right wing in the final, although sixteen-year-old Jimmy Mullen had played there in both the quarter and semi-finals. Stan had joined Wolves from Doncaster early in the 1938/39 season and had done tolerably well with 4 goals in 32 games, but within days of the defeat at Wembley he moved on to West Ham and became the first player ever to play in a League game for another side before the end of a season in which he had played in an FA Cup final. After the war, Stan had a useful spell with Peterborough, who were at that time in the Midland League.

Wolves' Glorious But Imperfect Season

PLAYERS APPRECIATED THEIR WARM HOMECOMING

By Nomad

SO we come to the end of another season. A glorious one for Wolves in many respects, yet how imperfect. The Molineux club have tasted the bitter truth of the axiom, "Beware when you are seeking championship and cup lest you win neither." As long as I live I shall remember my bitter disappointment over the 1939 F.A. Cup Final.

The season, however, has not ended without Wolves writing yet more football history—they are the first club to finish runners-up in both the cup and league championship.

I need not tell you how heart broken the side were at their failure at Wembley, but one and all they gave Portsmouth the highest praise for a fine display, which fully earned them the right to take the cup home.

I am informed, by the way, that the latest slogan is "Join the Navy and see the cup."

It would be impossible for me to let this moment pass without referring to the wonderful sportsmanship which the people of Wolverhampton have shown this week.

When we were coming home from London on Monday afternoon we told each other we would be lucky if there was as much as a taxi waiting the players when they stepped out of the train.

Yet the reception the lads got was overwhelming, and I can assure you that the players appreciated it.

All through the pleasures of the week-end in the Dorchester Hotel they had wilted at the thoughts of their return home. But when they got back they soon learned that, like themselves, their supporters could take defeat in the spirit they have taken the victories this season.

But surely this succession of honours just missed cannot go on. In two successive seasons the club have finished second in the table, while this time they failed at the last jump in the cup.

Wolves' supporters will be fully entitled to expect the club to go one better next time, and already Major Buckley is laying down his plans with the intention of bringing a major honour home next season.

The season has been a memorable one for the club. The number of victories has heavily outweighed the number of defeats, and Wolves have gained more First Division points than ever before.

My happiest memories of the campaign will be Wolves' 7—0 and 2—0 victories over Everton at Molineux; the splendid display of outside-left football given by Maguire when Wolves won 4—0 at Charlton; the fact that the club went from November 5th to March 8th, inclusive, with only one defeat, playing 23 matches, four of them in the cup; and Westcott's magnificent leadership for about two-thirds of the season.

I was also particularly pleased at the selection of Morris at right-back for England against Ireland and Scotland, but thought that Gardiner deserved more than one chance in a representative match.

Another special point of interest is the fact that Frank Taylor rose far above what anyone expected of him at left-back, and soon established himself as one of the soundest defenders in the team.

Surprise for Supporters

Tomorrow the club set out on a tour in which they will play matches in Norway and Holland. They deserve every bit of pleasure they can get out of it.

The news that Galley and Dorsett had not accepted the terms offered them by Wolves came as a first-class surprise to all the club's supporters.

It is not for me to enter into a discussion on Wolves domestic problems, but there will be much heart-burning in Wolverhampton and district until these two have signed.

Already Galley has been affected. Owing to the fact that a player who has not signed forms for his club cannot tour with the England team, the right-half has had to withdraw from the pleasure and experience the trip to Italy. Jugoslavia and Rumania would have given him. He has lost something like £40, the sum he would have received for his services.

In addition, Galley and Dorsett will not be able to go to Norway and Holland with their old club unless they sign forms in time, and it is to be hoped that the trouble will be smoothed over without delay.

Alterations at Molineux have been planned, and they will take place during the close season. Whether there will be alterations in the personnel as well I am not at liberty to say. My only remark in this connection is: Be prepared.

League appearances: Scott 40, Morris 39, Taylor 40, Parker 3, Galley 41, Cullis 39, Gardiner 37, Maguire 32, Thompson (now with Sunderland) 11, Westcott 36, Burton (now with West Ham) 28, Dorsett 35, Kirkham (now with Bournemouth) 5, McIntosh 33, Barlow (now with Portsmouth) 3, Wright 4, Myers 3, Mullen 7, McMahon 1, McAloon 2, Goddard 4, Steen 1, Sidlow 1, McDonald 2, Rooney 2, Brown 2, Tagg 1.

Goal-scorers: Westcott 32, Dorsett 26, Galley 11 (nine penalties), McIntosh 7, Burton 3, Kirkham 3, Maguire 2, Barlow 1, Steen 1, McAloon 1, Wright 1.

'Glorious but imperfect' was how a local newspaper described Wolves' last pre-war season. For a team enjoying such success, it is perhaps surprising to find that they used no fewer than twenty-seven players during the campaign. It is also interesting to note that Wolves got an 'overwhelming' reception when they returned to Wolverhampton on the Monday after the final. We shall never know whether they would have won a major honour in the following season, as war clouds were already descending and League football did not return for another seven seasons.

Three

The War Years

WOLVES FIRST TEAM LEAGUE FIXTURES, 1939-40.

Date	Name of Club	For Agst Pts	Date	Name of Club.	For Agst Pts.
Aug.26—	Arsenal	0-1...h	Dec. 26—	Sunderland	0-0...h
29—	Grimsby	4-2...a	30—	Blackpool	1-1...h
Sept. 2—	Blackpool	0-1...a	Jan. 6—	Brentford	1-0...a
6—	Aston Villa	2-1...h	13—	3rd Round F.A.Cup.	
9—	Brentford	5-2...h	20—	Blackburn R.	—...h
11—	Aston Villa	2-2...a	27—	Portsmouth	0-1...a
16—	Blackburn	—...a	Feb. 3—	Everton	7-0...h
23—	Portsmouth	3-0...h	10—	Huddersfield	2-1...a
30—	Everton	0-1...a	17—	Leeds U.	0-1...a
Oct. 7—	Huddersfield	3-0...h	24—	Stoke City	3-0...h
14—	Leeds United	4-1...h	Mar. 2—	Middlesbro'	0-1...a
21—	Stoke City	3-5...a	9—	Charlton A.	3-1...h
28—	Middlesbro'	6-1...h	16—	Sheffield U.	—...a
Nov. 4—	Charlton A.	4-0...a	23—	Preston N.E.	3-0...h
11—	Sheffield U.	—...h	25—	Derby C.	2-2...a
18—	Preston N.E.	2-4...a	26—	Derby C.	0-0...h
25—	Manch'er U.	3-0...h	30—	Manch'er U.	3-1...a
Dec. 2—	Liverpool	2-0...a	April 6—	Liverpool	2-2...h
9—	Bolton W.	1-1...h	13—	Bolton W.	0-0...a
16—	Chelsea	3-1...a	20—	Chelsea	2-0...h
23—	Arsenal	0-0...a	27—	(F.)	
25—	Sunderland	1-1...a	May 4—	Grimsby T.	5-0...h

WOLVES SECOND TEAM LEAGUE FIXTURES, 1939-40.

Date	Name of Club	For Agst Pts.	Date	Name of Club.	For Agst Pts
Aug.26--	Manch'er C.	1-1...a	Dec. 30—	Blackburn R.	4-1...a
Sept. 2—	Blackburn R.	4-1...h	Jan. 6—	Sheffield W.	2-0...h
4—	Aston Villa	2-3...a	13—	Chesterfield	2-0...h
9—	Sheffield W.	1-2...a	20—	Blackpool	1-1...a
13—	W. B. Albion	4-2...h	27—	Bury	1-4...h
16—	Blackpool	5-0...h	Feb. 3—	Everton	3-0...a
23—	Bury	2-2...a	10—	Huddersfield	1-2...h
30—	Everton	5-1...h	17—	Newcastle U.	0-0...h
Oct. 7—	Huddersfield	1-3...a	24—	Birmingham	1-1...a
14—	Newcastle U.	1-1...a	Mar. 2—	Stoke City	4-0...h
21—	Birmingham	1-0...h	9—	Manch'er U.	0-5...a
28—	Stoke City	0-2...a	16—	Sheffield U.	1-0...h
Nov. 4—	Manch'er U.	3-4...h	22—	Derby C.	1-0...a
11—	Sheffield U.	0-1...a	23—	Burnley	0-3...a
18—	Burnley	2-3...h	25—	Derby C.	2-1...h
25—	Preston N.E.	0-5...a	30—	Preston N.E.	2-1...h
Dec. 2—	Bolton W.	0-1...h	April 6—	Bolton W.	4-0...a
9—	Liverpool	2-1...a	13—	Liverpool	4-0...h
16—	Leeds U.	1-0...h	20—	Leeds U.	0-0...a
23—	Manch'er C.	2-4...h	27—	Aston Villa	2-1...h
25—	Chesterfield	0-1...a	May 4—	W. B. Albion	1-1...a

This is the fixture card for the season that never was. After just three games, in which Wolves drew 2-2 with Arsenal, 0-0 at Grimsby and lost 2-1 at Blackpool, war was declared and, following a three-week gap, football was reorganised into wartime regional leagues.

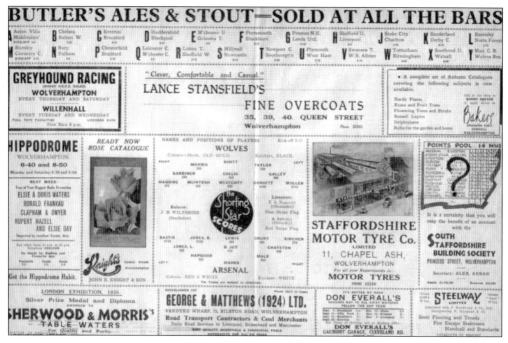

These were the line-ups for the opening game of 1939/40 when Wolves drew 2-2 with Arsenal at Molineux, with Dickie Dorsett and Dennis Westcott on the mark for Wolves and Reg Lewis and Alf Kirchen scoring for Arsenal. The result was, of course, deleted from the records when the Football League programme was abandoned a week later when war broke out, but it is interesting to note that when the game was played again in August 1946 on the resumption of League Football, Bill Morris, Stan Cullis, Tommy Galley, Dennis Westcott and Jimmy Mullen were again in the Wolves side and George Male, Bernard Joy, Reg Lewis and Cliff Bastin turned out for Arsenal. Wolves won the 1946 game 6-1, and they were watched by 50,845 fans compared with 41,222 in 1939, while Dennis Westcott for Wolves and Reg Lewis for Arsenal scored in both games.

Jimmy Mullen made his Wolves debut in February 1939 aged 16 years and 1 month. He played in an FA Cup semi-final one month later, but just missed out on an FA Cup final place. After 'Dizzy' Burton's move to West Ham, Jimmy was an automatic first choice at the start of 1939/40 and he played in 91 wartime games, scoring 27 goals. After the war, he took his tally of League and Cup goals to 112 in 486 games. After his retirement from football, Jimmy ran a sports shop in the town for many years.

THE WOLVES
Official Programme

Saturday, Nov. 18th, 1939. Kick-off 3 p.m.

NAMES AND POSITIONS OF PLAYERS.

WOLVES

Colours—Shirts, Old Gold.   Knickers, Black.

RIGHT   SCOTT   LEFT

PARKER   TAYLOR
(2)   (3)

GODDARD   GALLEY   GARDINER
(4)   (5)   (6)

STEEN   MULLEN   WESTCOTT   McINTOSH   WRIGHT, W.
(7)   (8)   (9)   (10)   (11)

Referee—   Linesmen—
T. SMITH   T. H. BUTTON (W-hampton)
(Atherstone)   Red Stripe
                            H. J. SILVESTER (W-hampton)
                                   Blue Stripe

TAYLOR   LOWRIE   GREEN   FIRTH   ASHALL
(11)   (10)   (9)   (8)   (7)

BOILEAU   CRAWLEY   SNAPE
(6)   (5)   (4)

METCALF   ASTLEY
(3)   (2)

LEFT   MORGAN   RIGHT

COVENTRY CITY

Colours—Shirts, Blue and White Vertical Stripes   Knickers, White

THE TEAMS ARE SUBJECT TO ALTERATION

FOOTBALL AT MOLINEUX GROUNDS

Birmingham Combination.

TAMWORTH

Saturday Next, Nov. 25th, 1939 Kick-off 2-45 p.m.

Soon Wolves were playing in the Midland section of the Wartime League, and for a time they were able to field most of their 1939 FA Cup final team – as this match programme (reduced by wartime conditions to a single sheet) indicates. It is also significant, however, that a certain fair-haired fifteen year old called Billy Wright featured in Wolves' line-up and, despite consistently being the youngest player on the field, he had scored 3 goals in 18 games by the end of that first wartime season.

WOLVES PRODUCE A MACHINE GUN

SIX "BULL'S-EYES" AGAINST BLUES

WOLVERHAMPTON W. 6, BIRMINGHAM 2

BIRMINGHAM were well and truly eclipsed by Wolverhampton Wanderers at Molineux to-day by six goals to two. Westcott claimed three, Dorsett (2) and Mullen (penalty) were the other scorers. Broome netted twice for Blues.

In the opening match of the war-time, Midland Regional competition, Birmingham beat Wanderers by three goals to two, at Molineux.

WOLVERHAMPTON WANDERERS.— Sidlow; Dowen, Taylor; Goddard, Galley; Gardiner; Steen, McIntosh, Westcott, Dorsett, Mullen.

BIRMINGHAM.—Hibbs; Quinton, Jennings; Bye, Turner, Iverson; Edwards, Dearson, Broome, Craven, Brown.

Referee: G. L. Iliffe, Leicester.

Wretched weather attended the match and when the players appeared there were barely 2,000 people present.

Wolves made the first raid on a rain-sodden ground and when Birmingham tried to get going Taylor checked a promising movement.

Next time Birmingham approached Brown shot wide.

It was not long before the Wanderers were seen on the attack again and McIntosh, from close quarters, lifted the ball over the bar.

Iverson stepped into the breach to stop another likely effort, on the part of the home forwards, and Birmingham replied with a pretty movement between Dearson, Bye and Edwards.

Finally the Villa man squared the ball nicely and Brown headed into the net, but before he did so, he was flagged for offside and no goal resulted.

Birmingham served up another strong attack, which came near to bringing a goal and Broome followed with a characteristic dash, only to be checked by Taylor in the penalty area.

LIVELY DISPLAY

Though the conditions were difficult, both teams provided lively football.

There was a little incident near the home goal when Sidlow got down to a swift shot from Edwards, who tried to recover the ball, whilst the 'keeper was on the ground, but the referee intervened as a home defender raced back, and then the home forwards returned to the attack.

Iverson put in some stout work during a period of further pressure by the Wanderers.

Broome and Dearson were responsible for a joint effort which gave the opposition trouble, and on the Wolves' next visit to the Birmingham end Westcott had the misfortune to stumble in the mud when he was clean through.

Each end was visited in rapid succession, and for the visitors Broome drove in a low shot which just missed the far post.

Wolves' reply was a hard shot from Dorsett, which Hibbs handled in customary style.

HOME SIDE GAIN LEAD.

Again Dorsett got through, but this time Iverson came to the rescue.

At the end of 25 minutes, however, the Wanderers gained the lead.

Receiving a nice pass from Dorsett, Westcott went forward with the ball and Jennings slipped before he could tackle.

Hibbs ran out in the hope of saving the situation, but WESTCOTT cleverly placed the ball inside the net.

Three minutes later Birmingham equalised in clever style.

Bye started the movement with a pass to Edwards, who in turn gave the ball to BROOME.

The centre-forward smartly eluded Taylor and then smashed the ball into the net, leaving Sidlow helpless.

Birmingham's goal had a narrow escape just afterwards.

A free-kick was awarded Wolves near the penalty area and Dorsett hit the far post with a rasping shot, Westcott failing to convert when the ball rebounded direct to him.

Turner did a powerful lot of work for Birmingham, in defence, and Galley was equally successful in the corresponding position for Wanderers, who had to submit to a spell of defensive play.

Dowen got his side out of trouble when Dearson came across to give a hand to Brown.

A few minutes before the interval Westcott had to leave the field, apparently, a twisted knee, but he had hardly disappeared from view when the Wanderers took the lead again, DORSETT scoring with a hard shot at 40 minutes, after good work in company with McIntosh.

Birmingham made a spirited reply, but Broome headed wide from Edwards' pass and Brown followed with a bold dash only to be foiled at the last moment by Dowen.

The football from both sets of forwards possessed plenty of snap and the day was keenly contested, being at all times interesting.

Half-time:—Wolverhampton .. 2
Birmingham .. 1

Westcott resumed in his normal

The ball went to Brown who did his best in difficult circumstances, but he was unable to find the net.

After Steen had once narrowly missed the same player put over a first-class centre and Westcott headed direct to Hibbs.

Wolves now played with great spirit and Hibbs again had to save from the home centre-forward.

Wolves secured a somewhat lucky third goal at 57 minutes.

Turner had stopped Westcott close in, but kicked against DORSETT'S legs, and the ball rebounded into the open goal, Hibbs having come out to join in the challenge.

A little feeling crept into the play at this point, and the referee awarded the Wanderers a penalty for a foul upon Dorsett.

MULLEN made no mistake with his aim from the spot kick, and scored a fourth goal at 65 minutes.

A minute later a through pass was smartly snapped up by WESTCOTT who went through to score with a neat shot.

At 68 minutes the same player, receiving a pass from McIntosh, scored a sixth goal and as the

DENNIS WESTCOTT
—in goal-scoring mood netted three times for Wolves against Blues.

score indicates the Wanderers were well on top in this half.

Birmingham were kept in their own half and had all their work cut out to hold the lively home raiders, but a picture goal came in reply for Birmingham.

Dearson gave a lovely pass to Edwards, who returned a perfect centre and BROOME placed the ball home at 75 minutes.

The Wolves were given a second penalty for another foul on Dorsett, but this time Mullen shot within range of Hibbs, who saved the penalty kick.

Birmingham had a very unhappy time in this half, but they fought back with spirit, though the odds were all against them, and in the closing stages made some lively attacks on the home goal.

It was Birmingham's second defeat in this competition, and quite their worst experience in Midland Regional football.

Result—Wolves 6
Birmingham 2

NEXT SATURDAY'S FOOTBALL

Midland.— Birmingham v. Walsall; Leicester v. Luton; Northampton v. Wolverhampton; West Bromwich Albion v. Coventry.

North-East—Middlesbrough v. Darlington.

South "A".—Arsenal v. Southend; Charlton v. Watford; Clapton v. West Ham; Crystal P. v. Millwall; Norwich v. Tottenham.

South "B".—Aldershot v. Southampton; Bournemouth v. Chelsea; Fulham v. Brentford; Portsmouth v. Reading; Q.P. Rangers v. Brighton.

South-West—Bristol C. v. Plymouth; Newport v. Bristol R.; Swansea v. Cardiff; Torquay v. Swindon.

Lancashire Cup.—Accrington v. Oldham; Blackburn v. Everton; Bury v. Blackpool; Liverpool Cup—New Brighton v. Southport.

Welsh Cup—Wrexham v. Wellington T.

Friendly Matches.—Barnsley v. Bradford; Bradford C. v. Rotherham; Burnley v. Manchester C.; Chester v. Bury; Chesterfield v. Halifax; Crewe v. Shrewsbury; Doncaster v. Huddersfield Town; Grimsby v. Leeds; Hull v. Notts County; Liverpool v. Preston; Manchester United v. Sheffield United; Newcastle v. Royal Artillery; Nottingham Forest v. Stockport; Rochdale v. Tranmere; Port Vale v. West Bromwich; Sheffield Wednesday v. Stoke.

SCOTTISH LEAGUE.

East and North-East.— Arbroath v. Hibernian; Dundee v. King's Park; Dunfermline v. Alloa; East Fife v. Stenhousemuir; Falkirk v. Raith; Hearts v. Aberdeen; St. Bernards v. Dundee U.; St. Johnstone v. Cowdenbeath.

Western—Airdrieonians v. Partick; Ayr v. St. Mirren; Celtic v. Third Lanark; Morton v. Hamilton; Motherwell v. Dumbarton; Queen of South v. Kilmarnock; Queen's Park v. Clyde; Rangers v. Albion.

WEST BROMWICH HOSPITAL

Whit Crowd-Out: Wolves Travel In Guard's Van!

NEVER have the Wolves travelled under such trying conditions to play an important game as they did yesterday and today. They left Wolverhampton at 4.15 yesterday afternoon and arrived in Leeds, where they stopped overnight, at 10.45 a.m.

From Birmingham to the Yorkshire city the Wolves players and the small party travelled in the guards van, their only seats the luggage they carried, telephones the "Express and Star" special representative with the team.

This morning the party made an early start to York, and for this portion of the journey they stood in a crowded corridor. Their position was even worse during the next stage to Durham, and all had to stand packed like sardines in corridors and vestibules between carriages.

The actual travelling time on the train was about 11 hours, and so the players, who hold the opinion that half the population of the Midlands was travelling north to spend the Whitsun holiday, were certainly anything but as "fresh as daisies" when they walked on to the pitch

HOMEWARD BOUND WORKERS CROWD PLATFORMS

Thousands of workers, intent upon leaving Birmingham for a Whitsun break at their homes all over the country, crowded on to Birmingham station platforms from late last night.

Early this morning there was still a queue outside the booking office at the L.M.S. station, and London bound trains and the north bound platforms were crowded.

Despite this rush of traffic, however, both stations reported that no passengers up till noon had been refused a journey.

There were queues at all bus stops from which buses left for the nearer "holiday" spots, but an official said that the traffic was such that they hoped to deal with all returning passengers comfortably, unless they all chose to come back on the last bus!

WULFRUNIANS ARE REASONABLE

Indications are that in the main Wolverhampton people are responding reasonably well to the Government's request not to travel this Whitsuntide.

At this town's G.W.R. and L.M.S.

stations an *Express and Star* reporter was told that while trains have been well loaded there has been no serious overcrowding.

Of course, it is impossible to say whether these conditions will remain the same throughout Whitsuntide.

Neither of the railways has experienced any difficulty so far in catering for the travelling public. No extra trains or excursions will be run.

It is not expected that road traffic will be increased this weekend.

The bicycle has come into its own, however, and here and there today one could see merry groups of young cyclists making their way to the country.

Owing to petrol shortage it is unlikely travelling will be much reduced by car, and from this point of view this is likely to be the quietest Whitsuntide for many years.

CLOSE DOWN

Of 12 Wolverhampton firms approached by the *Express and Star* today the works of six will be closed down only on Monday. Five closed at noon today until Tuesday morning, and one is also having Tuesday off. Some of them will have skeleton staffs working during the holiday.

Passenger traffic at all the London terminal stations was described as "even smaller than the average week-end," an official said "there is no doubt that people are trying to co-operate helpfully."

Even the dog wanted a ticket for the second leg of the Cup Final when Wolves meet Sunderland at Molineux next Saturday. There was a good number of women in the queue which formed this morning.

Wolves Strong Favourites For League War Cup

WOLVES certainly earned the right to become favourites for the Football League War Cup as a result of the drawn game at Sunderland in the first leg of the final.

This thrill-packed struggle, watched by 35,000 spectators, almost ended in a victory for the home eleven, but Westcott made things level with a grand goal in the last few minutes.

Immediately afterwards Wolves got the ball into the net through Mullen, but the referee ruled that the winger was offside.

The crowd sighed with relief, but this was not the last thrill. Sunderland swept down the field, Stubbins shot, and the ball hit the inside of the upright to rebound into Sidlow's waiting arms.

When referee J. Wiltshire, now a corporal in the R.A.F., blew for time, everyone appeared satisfied with the result.

TYPICAL WESTCOTT GOAL

Wolves started as if they would carry everything before them. Their attack combined well, and in the tenth minute Westcott put them ahead with a grand shot from an acute angle.

He worked the ball over to the left, and he almost scored from the wing position. It was a typical Westcott effort.

The first half was Wolves, although Sunderland had their share of the play, but their attack lacked punch and initiative in front of goal.

A complete change came over the game in the second half, which undoubtedly was Sunderland's.

Their forwards played much better, and in the last quarter of an hour they strove hard to increase their 2-1 lead, the goals being notched by Carter and Stubbins.

DEFENCE HELD OUT

However, Wolves' defence held out, Galley, Robinson and Dowen being called upon to make numerous hefty clearances. Sidlow, too, had a busy time.

One thing everyone agreed upon—it was one of the best cup ties seen at Roker Park for many a day.

All Wolves players gave a good account of themselves. Galley, as usual, was the mainstay of the defence, but although he worked hard his display was not as spectacular as that in the return match with the Albion at Molineux.

His splendid through passes and clever shadowing of Whitelum, Sunderland's leader, were features of the game.

SIDLOW LIKE A ROCK

Sidlow, too, earned a special word of praise. He gave a brilliant performance and stood like a rock between the Sunderland attackers and his goal.

He could not be blamed for either goal, and the second shot would have deceived anyone. The high ball appeared to be going round the upright, but it suddenly swerved into the corner of the net.

Dowen and Robinson had a hard period after half-back after playing inside-forward in both semi-finals and scoring three goals.

Thornhill and Dorsett, the wing

halves, worked well, and towards the end Dorsett went down so heavily with a foot injury that he appeared to have received a bad knock; however, he was soon back to help keep at bay the lively Sunderland attackers.

WESTCOTT ALWAYS READY

Young Jimmy Mullen, fresh from his introduction to army life, was the better winger, but he had far more to do than Broome, who for a long period seldom got hold of the ball.

McIntosh weaved the ball about in dazzling fashion, Stevenson showed improved form, but it was Westcott who was the real danger.

He never let a single opportunity slip by; he worried the Sunderland defence every time he went for the ball. Westcott has now scored 13 goals in the competition.

On this display, Wolves should win the return game. It is to be hoped that Major Buckley can get together a full side for the second game, with Taylor back in the team.

"NIGHTMARE" JOURNEY

Due consideration must be given to the Wolves' players for their wonderful fight following their long journey. From Birmingham to Leeds they travelled in the guard's van, sitting on leather bags and odds and the second part of the journey, on the morning of the match, was a nightmare.

Packed like sardines, they stood in crowded corridors until reaching Durham, it certainly did not help to keep them fresh for the match.

The journey was not without its humour, and the Wolves did not go hungry, despite the "no-food-at-holidays" rule laid down by the railway companies.

Bill Hill produced sandwiches and cakes out of a huge grip from time to time. The bag should now be dubbed, "Pandora's Box"!

GALLEY SLEPT ON MAIL BAGS

It was during the journey to Leeds that Galley, McIntosh, and Dorsett gave a spot of help to the busy railway staff. They helped put in mail bags, bicycles, and parcels, which were stacked in the already packed van.

Galley finished the journey by falling asleep full length on the mail bags, using a basket of watercress as a pillow!

What a contrast to their last cup final journey to Wembley, when their first-class saloon gave the Wolves' party lavish comfort and food.

This, however, was the War Cup, and the players travelled at Whitsun, when every train bound for the north was packed to the last inch of space.

Albion Beat Walsall Easily

There was an end-of-the-season flavour about the Albion-Walsall match at The Hawthorns, but it had its bright patches.

Albion merited their 3—1 win after Newsome, an Albion player, had put Walsall in front.

Bowen equalised before the interval, and Elliott and Ashley made simple second-half goals following bad defensive mistakes by Walsall.

Wolves closed down for the 1940/41 season having made a loss on 1939/40, but they were back with a vengeance in 1941/42 when they won the Football League War Cup, beating Sunderland 6-3 on aggregate in the two-legged final. Conditions were tough for both players and fans, but Wolves pulled off a fine 2-2 draw at Roker Park in the first leg.

Major Frank Buckley with Tom Galley and the Football League War Cup.

"Wolves A Grand Side,"

Says Sunderland Manager

SINCEREST tribute to Wolves' magnificent War Cup victory at Molineux on Saturday was paid by Manager W. Murray, of Sunderland, when I saw him after the game (writes our special football correspondent).

"Wolves thoroughly deserved their success," he told me as he hurriedly ate a meal to catch an early train back. "They are a grand side, and my boys were well beaten."

League president, Mr. W. C. Cuff, also expressed a similar view when he handed Tom Galley, Wolves' captain, the cup.

Tom was very modest about his side's success. He said, all smiles. "I think we deserve this cup, and I thank you very much!"

WESTCOTT'S USUAL

After watching last week's game at Roker Park I was never in doubt about the issue, and although Sunderland never gave up trying, even when three goals down, their attacks were never as much on the mark as the Wolves.

Westcott did the usual by opening the scoring. This was his 14th goal of the competition proper, and it was a splendid effort, the Wolves leader getting the ball from Broome's perfect pass.

Broome notched the second point after a typical swift run down his wing. This was the Villa winger's best game for Wolves in the cup, and without any doubt he was the fastest winger on the field.

The second half, which was fought out at a faster pace than the first.

was in its 15th minute when Carter reduced the lead from Stubbins's dribble, which started in his own half. It was a well-earned goal.

It looked as though Sunderland would be more in the game with this success, but the Wolves quickly took command again, and Rowley, the Manchester United but Wolverhampton-born player, added two more goals.

SIDLOW'S FINE PLAY

I thought Stubbins was Sunderland's best and hardest-working forward.

Praise must be handed to Sidlow, Wolves' goalkeeper, for a truly wonderful performance. He saved many terrific drives, some from point-blank range, and his anticipation was perfect.

He was cool and efficient, and had complete understanding with his backs. On the other hand, Heywood, too, was a good goalkeeper but at times he was flurried.

McIntosh weaved the ball about well in a quiet-but-effortless style. Mullen was not quite so good as last week, and Rowley, who on his last appearance for Wolves scored five goals, was a schemer of merit.

TRIBUTE TO GALLEY

Galley gave another brilliant performance. His work was never spectacular, but no one worked harder. Tom is without doubt the best centre-half in the country today.

Dorsett and Robinson were good wing halves, and the first-named was at his best in the second half when he fed the men in front with plenty of excellent through passes.

Wolves won well. They finished as fresh as they started, and are now looking forward to meeting Brentford, the London Cup winners, at Stamford Bridge on Saturday.

Although only a few hundreds of Sunderland supporters travelled to the game, the crowd of 43,038, who paid £4,552, cheered their effort just as much as the home eleven.

Wolves have played ten games in the competition proper against Chester, Manchester United, Manchester City, Albion and Sunderland. They have scored 25 goals and ten have been registered by their opponents.

"T" Division (Bushbury) wardens meet N.F.S. "A" in the first round of Wolverhampton Civil Defence Sports Association cricket knock-out tomorrow night on Courtaulds ground. On Wednesday, Fordhouses play the Wardens "A" team on Fordhouses ground in the first-named of Wolverhampton and district knock-out. Both matches begin at 7 p.m.

PRICE   -   ONE PENNY

THE WOLVES
Official Programme

Saturday, May 30th, 1942. Kick-off 3-0 p.m.
Football League Cup—FINAL.

NAMES AND POSITIONS OF PLAYERS.

WOLVES
Colours—Shirts, Old Gold.   Knickers, Black.

RIGHT   SIDLOW   LEFT
                (1)   TAYLOR.
          DOWEN   ROBINSON
           (2)   (3)
  ROBINSON
  THORNHILL   GALLEY   DORSETT
    (4)   (5)   (6)
                                ROWLEY.
BROOME McINTOSH WESTCOTT STEVENSON MULLEN
  (7)   (8)   (9)   (10)   (11)

Referee—   Linesmen—
Cpl. J. M. WILTSHIRE   Red Stripe
     (R.A.F.)   A. BAKER (Crewe)
                            Blue Stripe
                          A. SEWELL (Coventry)

ROBINSON CARTER WHITELUM STUBBINS SPUHLER
  (11)   (10)   (9)   (8)   (7)

HASTINGS   HEWISON   HOUSAM
  (6)   (5)   (4)

    EVES   GORMAM
    (3)   (2)

LEFT   HEYWOOD   RIGHT
               (1)

SUNDERLAND
Colours—Shirts, Red and White.   Knickers, Black.

THE TEAMS ARE SUBJECT TO ALTERATION. SUNDERLAND 2 CARTER

WOLVES 4 ROWLEY 2 BROOME 1 WESTCOTT

43,038 were at Molineux for the second leg to see Wolves win a tremendous game 4-2, with a side that included three 'guest' players. Jack Dowen and Jack Rowley were former Wolves men who were by then on the books of Hull City and Manchester United respectively, while Frank Broome was registered with Aston Villa.

The war years inevitably brought tragedy as well as triumph for Wolves. Eric Robinson, who played with distinction in the 1942 War Cup triumph, drowned just three months later while taking part in military exercises in the River Derwent. He was just twenty-three years old.

A year later Joe Rooney, who had played in first-team games against Aston VIlla and Charlton in April 1939, was killed in action in Italy aged just twenty-four.

WOLVES' BIGGEST DEFEAT OF SEASON

By THE PILGRIM

Wolves crashed heavily at Crewe to the tune of 8—1, their biggest defeat of the season. At half-time, when the home team were leading 4—1, the score flattered them, but at the end there was no question of their superiority in all departments.

Crewe's goals were scored by Dyer (4), Wardell (2), Anderson and Hewitt. Gardiner got Wolves' solitary point from a penalty.

As Sidlow was playing in a special charity game, Wolves brought in Bilton, who has played for several clubs this season. Bilton has never played worse for Wolves. His anticipation was at fault with at least four of the goals.

RICHARDSON'S "300" FOR ALBION

By scoring twice in the league match at Walsall, Billy Richardson, who has been with Albion for 14 years, brought his bag of goals to 300, truly a remarkable record.

Albion's other scorers were Eric Jones and A. J. Evans. Apart from Richardson's efforts to get his 300th goal—it came just before the end—there was little enthusiasm, and both attacks were rather erratic.

As was anticipated, Aston Villa were beaten at Blackpool in the first leg of the Football League War Cup semi-final.

Blackpool, with a 3—1 lead, have an excellent chance of reaching the final, especially if they have the assistance of Dodds and Matthews at Villa Park on Saturday.

Farrow, Finan, and Dix were Blackpool's marksmen. Davis replied for Villa.

Wolves Reserves travelled to Ludlow to play a special charity game. Wolves lost 3—1.

Rowley's Eight Is A Record For Molineux

BY THE PILGRIM.

Rowley.

WOLVERHAMPTON - BORN Jack Rowley, the Manchester United centre-forward now on leave from the army, dazzled Derby's defence with his brilliant leadership at Molineux on Saturday and created a ground record by scoring all his side's eight goals. Wolves won 8—1.

This was the biggest tonic Major Buckley has offered to his young side this season, and after Rowley's first goal in the third minute the young forwards went into the game with relish.

Rowley has been playing well for Distillery, the Irish club, this season, for whom he has only failed to score on two occasions.

TO SETTLE ARGUMENTS

Saturday's scoring record has caused a lot of controversy in the town, so the following information should settle many arguments.

Rowley scored five goals for Wolves last season against Everton. He got two more in the cup final against Sunderland. His previous best was for Manchester United against New Brighton. United won 13—1, and Rowley notched seven. This was Rowley's first appearance for Wolves this season. I hope it will not be his last, but, unfortunately, he will be unable to play at Derby next Saturday. Neither will Sidlow, who is booked for a representative match.

Rowley's eight goals came at the following times: Three, 14, 17, 36, 51, 82, 84 and 85 minutes—four in each half. Not only did he show his prowess as an individualist, but he distributed the ball freely and accurately.

WOLVES' BEST DISPLAY

Without doubt this was Wolves' best display of the season. Every player showed grand form; there was not a weak spot in the eleven. As usual, Sidlow gave a good account of himself in goal, Galley played a quiet but striking game, and Roberts and Crook worked hard and successfully on the left wing. Lyman scored for Derby nine minutes from the end. On the whole, Derby disappointed with their weak finishing, but there were periods when their positional play was delightful—until they got into the penalty area.

Official attendance: 4,594.

POOR SHOOTING AT HAWTHORNS

Albion played well enough to beat Walsall except that the inside forwards lacked punch and direction. Williams did not have as much to do as would be imagined from the home side's territorial advantage, but he did his work well and at least two of his saves were outstanding. Albion, however, had enough chances to win.

It was the sixth match out of 13 in which Albion had failed to score.

Walsall defenders were entitled to some of the credit. They stuck to their task well. In the circumstances it would not have been surprising had Walsall taken both points, but their forwards were off the mark too, while not having the chances of their opponents.

15,000 AT VILLA PARK

Before the day's biggest crowd (15,000) Villa beat Birmingham at Villa Park by the odd goal of three. Birmingham had slightly the better of the first half, but Villa were well on top after the interval and might have won by a large margin. Birmingham scored through Gutteridge, who headed through his own goal, while Villa's leader, Davis, who gave a good display, notched both goals for his side.

Goals flowed more freely in games played during the Second World War than at any other time in Wolves' history: in the space of five months in 1942/43 they beat Derby 8-1 at Molineux and lost 8-1 to Crewe at Gresty Road.

Joe Gardiner was in Wolves' defence in both the 8-1 defeat at Crewe and the 8-1 win over Derby. He signed from Bearpark in 1934 and played in 139 matches before the war, including the 1939 FA Cup final. After the war, he served Wolves as trainer and scout until the 1980s.

While Jack Rowley, who scored all eight goals in that win over Derby, went on to star for Manchester United and England after the war, Don Bilton, who was on the wrong end of that 8-1 hammering at Crewe, never actually played a Football League game. During the war years he was one of twelve different 'keepers to appear for Wolves, totalling six games for them without being on the winning side. He also played for Derby, Notts County, Stoke and Walsall in wartime games and after the war gave good service to a number of local non-League clubs, including Bilston and Darlaston.

WOLVES BOY WINGER'S DASH

By THE PILGRIM

FOOTBALL history was made at Molineux this afternoon when 14-year-old Buchanan, youngest player ever to play in first-class football, appeared on the Wolves right wing.

Buchanan, who is 5ft. 6in. and turns the scale at 9½st. is at present continuing his education at Wolverhampton. He started to play when eight years old, and, although so young, has appeared in a representative match at Hampden Park, where he scored two goals.

Wolves made several changes, Stan. Cullis reappearing at centre-half, and Westcott led the attack.

Morby was brought in at right-back, and Springthorpe made his first appearance as a forward at outside-left.

Three of the Albion players—Jones, Chapman and Witcombe—were making their first appearance of the season Teams :—

WOLVES : Sidlow; Morby, Ashton; Wright, Cullis, Thornhill; Buchanan, Crook, Westcott, Alderton, Springthorpe.

ALBION : Adams; Parker (A.), Shaw; Millard (L.), Sankey, Witcombe; Elliott, Chapman, Jones, Evans, McDonald.

About 8,000 spectators saw Wolves make a quick attack and force a fruitless corner in the first minute, the move coming from Buchanan, who showed great dash

Albion then made three swift attacks, but their inside forwards were well held by Ashton and Cullis, who cleared cleanly and accurately.

First big thrill came when Buchanan finished a glorious run with a perfect centre.

Westcott dashed in and had the misfortune to see the ball from his header strike the cross-bar, with Adams on his knees.

Misunderstanding by Wolves defenders let Elliott through, but as Sidlow left his goal the Albion winger shot wide and missed a first-class opportunity.

When Jones was brought down by Ashton Albion were awarded a free kick on the fringe of the penalty area, but the danger was eased with no difficulty.

Buchanan again came into the limelight with another splendid centre, and from it Parker just managed to clear almost off the goal line.

Wolves boy winger was certainly making an impressive debut in first division football

In Wolves' next raid Westcott snapped up a through pass, but shot straight into Adams' arms. Wolves leader should have scored, for he was well placed

At the other end Jones struck the upright, and from the clearance Westcott went near with a low drive

Sidlow, who was playing well, saved in brilliant fashion from Jones's capital header and from another Buchanan centre Westcott tried hard, only for Adams to rush out and clear. Half-time—Wolves 0, Albion 0.

When the game was resumed Alderton and Crook changed positions, Springthorpe went to right-back, and Morby to outside-left.

Westcott troubled Adams with a high ball, and in the next minute had another tussle with the Albion goalkeeper.

Wolves hit the headlines in September 1942 when they fielded Scottish-born winger Cameron Buchanan in a wartime game against West Brom aged 14 years and 2 months. He went on to play in 18 wartime games and to score 6 goals. After the war, he had spells with Bournemouth and Norwich, playing in almost 100 League games but never quite fulfilling his early promise. He did, however, move successfully into the laundry business and it has been good to see him at former players' reunions at Molineux in recent times.

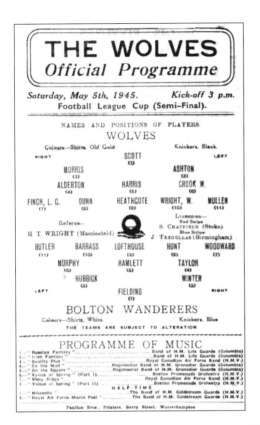

1945 Semi-Final Souvenir
PRICE 6d.
All proceeds to Wolverhampton Civic and "Express and Star"
Comforts Fund Special Victory Appeal

Moir Scores For Bolton Just Before Interval

Wolves were again on the Wartime Cup trail in 1944/45 and reached the semi-final before going out 4-3 on aggregate after two fiercely contested games against Bolton Wanderers. This was the souvenir produced to mark the occasion, and a remarkable feature of the games was that the Second World War officially ended halfway between the first leg and the second leg and that Dennis Westcott, straight from serving in the army at Bremen, led Wolves' attack in the first leg and Alex Mcintosh, who had been reported missing believed killed a few weeks earlier, returned from a prisoner of war camp to play in the second leg.

By THE PILGRIM

IT will be a long time before Wolves will have such an easy victory as they registered at Molineux this afternoon against Lovells' Athletic, who went down to the tune of eight goals to one.

The visitors' defence could do little against Mullen and Wright, England's new left wing, and all the forwards found the net.

Jennings, in the visitors' goal, although beaten eight times, played magnificently, and Clarke (H.), their centre-half, did well against Galley, who was also in exceptionally strong form.

The goals came in the following order: Mullen 2 minutes, Galley 30, Dunn 42, Wright 52, King 70, Wright 75, and Galley 80 and 82.

Prangley got a consolation goal for Lovell's direct from a free kick three minutes before the end. Wolves won on the aggregate by 12 goals to three.

Despite the bad weather there were 12,000 spectators.

The "Toffee" team, who travelled by road this morning, made changes, Witcomb, brother of the Albion player, being at inside-left, as Clarke (A.) is suffering from influenza.

Clark led the attack instead of Phillips, who is now awaiting embarkation leave, and Fischer came in for Hardwicke, injured in the first "leg."

In all, Lovells fielded seven amateurs, including the whole of their forward line.

Wolves made two changes, Kelly being at right-back in place of Morris, who was unable to make the journey, and Mullen appeared at outside-left.

Teams:

WOLVES.—Williams; Kelly, Ashton; Alderton, McLean, Crook; King, Dunn, Galley, Wright, Mullen.

LOVELLS. — Jennings; Slattery, Whitehouse; Prangley, Clarke (H.) Bye; Williams, Fisher, Clark, Witcomb, Morgan.

Referee: G. H. Hann (Glastonbury)

Galley, who captained Wolves, won the toss, and elected to defend the hotel goal. There was a sensa-

MORE BIG CUP-TIE GATES

SOME of the attendances at today's second-leg cup-ties:—

Everton v. Preston	25,000
Albion v. Cardiff	15,000
Arsenal v. West Ham	25,000
Man. Utd. v. Accrington	15,000
York v. Chesterfield	15,000
Crystal P. v. Q.P.R.	15,000
Portsmouth v. B'ingham	30,000
Sunderland v. Grimsby	20,000
Derby v. Luton	18,000
Middlesbrough v. Leeds	22,000
Blackburn v. Bolton	20,000
Barnsley v. Newcastle	25,000

tional start, for Wolves took the lead after two minutes This followed two quick raids, in one of which Galley had gone close with a low drive.

MULLEN was the scorer, and he nipped in to reach a free kick and find the net with a well-directed shot.

Another Wolves thrust which the visiting defenders failed completely to stop, saw King lob the ball over to Wright, who however, was yards wide with a slow header.

HEADED FROM LINE

King was in action again with a terrific drive which Jennings managed to punch round the post, and from the corner Slattery headed off the line with the Lovell's goalkeeper well out of position.

The first time Lovell's were in action was when Williams got away on the right wing, but his namesake in the Wolves goal had no difficulty in stopping a rather weak shot.

Lovells defence was in trouble again when Galley moved over to the left-hand side of the penalty area, but Slattery blocked his shot to relieve the danger.

Mullen went near again, the ball being stopped at the expense of a corner, and then McLean was in the right position to stop a good movement between Williams and Fischer.

Two minutes later Williams left his goal to save from the advancing Morgan, following which McLean had an exciting tussle with Clark before kicking the ball upfield.

ANOTHER LET OFF

The last five minutes had seen a marked improvement in the visitors tactics, but their defence found Wolves forwards very fast in all their work.

Lovells had another let off when King weaved his way to the defence and struck the foot of an upright. From the rebound Jennings had difficulty in saving from Mullen.

Then Ashton stopped Clark as the Lovells centre-forward was making progress down the middle, and from the clearance King, who was playing remarkably well, almost found the mark with a swift header.

SECOND BY GALLEY

GALLEY increased Wolves' lead at 30 minutes, when he beat Jennings will a well-placed shot after receiving a long pass from Kelly.

It was not long before the ball was in Lovell's net again, but Wright, who was the marksman, was ruled offside after Jennings, who was playing brilliantly, had saved at point-blank range from Mullen.

England's new left wing was in dazzling form, and King, too, was contributing to the full with some excellent centres.

Lovell's had another narrow escape when from Mullen's strong centre, Galley skimmed the crossbar with a capital header.

Wolves went further ahead after 42 minutes. Galley started a fast movement by flicking the ball to Mullen. The winger pushed it through to DUNN, who made no mistake when exceptionally well placed.

In the closing stages Jennings saved a 45-yard drive from Ashton and with the last kick of the half

1945/46 was an intermediate season before football returned to normal in August 1946. Wolves finished sixth in the League South (comprised of First and Second Division teams from the Midlands and South), but the FA Cup was virtually back to normal, the only difference being that all ties were played on a two-legged home and away basis. This brought Wolves into conflict with Welsh team Lovells Athletic, whom they beat 4-2 at Lovells ground in Newport and 8-1 at Molineux.

Bill Morris was the only player apart from Tom Gulley to appear in the 1939 FA Cup final and in Wolves' first post-war FA Cup tie against Lovells. He had joined Wolves from Halesowen in 1933. He won 3 England caps and played 197 League and Cup games for Wolves and 68 wartime games for Wolves and another 22 for Wrexham.

DEFENCES STRONG IN INTERNATIONAL

By THE PILGRIM

HALF-TIMES

Wolves made a major signing in September 1945 when they managed to secure goalkeeper Bert Williams from Walsall for just £3,500. He had already been capped by England in a wartime international and soon he was figuring in an England v. Wales game at West Brom in May 1945 (when Wolves' other goalkeeper Cyril Sidlow was in the Welsh goal). While Bert stayed to play in 420 games for Wolves and to win 24 England caps Cyril moved on to Liverpool in February 1946 for £4,000 and went on to play 165 games for them and to win 7 Welsh caps.

Three of the players who emerged from the junior ranks during the war and went on to give great service in Wolves' First Division team in the 1940s. Angus McLean (bottom left) was a 'Bevin Boy' at Hilton Main Colliery who played in 125 wartime games and 158 games after the war, figuring initially in midfield then in every defensive position and occasionally up front. In 1967/68, he succeeded Brian Clough as manager of Hartlepool and took them to promotion from the Fourth Division. Roy Pritchard (top left), another Bevin Boy, was a right or left flank defender who played in 23 wartime games plus many reserve games, when he lined up alongside Johnny Paxton (with Dennis Parsons in goal to complete the three 'P's). After the war, he played in the 1949 FA Cup team, bravely playing on after being injured in the semi-final against Manchester United. He totalled 223 post-war games for Wolves before moving, via Aston Villa, to Notts County. Ray Chatham (top right) was a draughtsman by trade and played for Wolves as a part-timer. In wartime games he played as a striker, scoring 16 goals in 32 games, but after the war he was converted to a central defender, playing in 86 games up to 1954, when he moved to Notts County (linking up again a few years later with Roy Pritchard).

Four
The Glory Years of the 1950s and '60s

The public practice match at the start of the 1946/47 season introduced Wolves fans to some new signings, including two of the greatest players in their history: Jesse Pye, the striker from Notts County, and Johnny Hancocks, the winger from Walsall. Jesse went on to score 95 goals in 209 games before moving to Luton in 1952 and Johnny scored 168 goals in 378 games before moving to Wellington as player-manager in 1957.

Wolves Press On For The Title, If—

TERRIER IN WOLVES DEN

L OWLY Charlton got no change out of league leaders Wolves at Molineux today, and goals by Mullen (10 minutes) and Westcott (28) enabled the home side to strengthen their championship prospects, always providing, of course, that the league decide to carry on with the season's programme after May 10th.

Charlton, F.A. Cup semi-finalists, played well and had their chances, but there was no denying Wolves' right to the points.

A snowstorm, and the touch-lines were swept clear while the match was in progress.

By THE PILGRIM

It was not until shortly after midday that the match was declared "on." Ice had formed on the hard playing surface, and two players kicked a ball about for Referee W. E. Wood, of Luton, before he made his decision.

Tons of sand were used on the pitch, and a thin covering of grit proved beneficial.

With Cullis still unfit following his collapse at Middlesbrough last week, Galley came in at centre-half for Wolves, with Alderton at right-half and Wright, fresh from his triumph in Paris on Wednesday, at left-half.

Charlton made one change. Lancelotte taking the place of Dawson at inside-right, Young.

WOLVES. — Williams; McLean, Crook; Alderton, Galley, Wright; Hancocks, Ramscar, Westcott, Forbes, Mullen.

CHARLTON—Bartram; Croker, Shreeve; Johnson, Phipps, Welsh; Hurst, Lancelotte, Robinson (W.), Fenton, Duffy.

Referee: W. E. Wood (Luton).

There were about 35,000 spectators present when the teams took the field.

Galley, who captained Wolves, won the toss and elected to attack the Molineux goal.

FIRST-MINUTE SAVE

Charlton immediately got away on the left and Duffy put the ball over to Robinson, but the latter's hard shot, from close range, was saved in magnificent style by Williams. As the Wolves goalie pushed the ball away Hurst dashed in, but was unable to get to an effective drive.

Wolves quickly retaliated, and after Wright had just missed from 20 yards, a shot from Forbes was well handled by Bartram.

Despite the firmer surface, both teams were making good progress, but in one rash endeavour she full five yards on his back in an effort to reach a through pass from Fenton.

Mullen had a cross shot saved by Bartram, and at the other end Williams had to give all the foot of the post to clear an unexpected effort from Welsh.

Another Wolves attack ended with Forbes, who slipped as he shot, putting the ball over the crossbar, and then Galley was prominent in stopping a strong Charlton raid.

Two more Wolves attacks followed, and they were rewarded in the second when Mullen opened the scoring after ten minutes.

The movement was started by Alderton, who gave the ball to Ramscar. Hampered by Welsh the inside forward passed to Alderton's hard drive.

Hancocks, and from the winger's cross, centre MULLEN got the ball first time and gave Bartram no chance with a low and powerful drive.

Charlton, South's sole representative in this season's F.A. Cup semi-finals, were playing attractive football. Most of their danger came from the wingmen, who were showing plenty of dash and getting in many dangerous centres.

Wolves added to their lead in the 28th minute, when, from a glorious through pass by Ramscar, WESTCOTT shot into the corner of the net from 15 yards.

Real winter conditions now prevailed, for snow was falling heavily.

RAMSCAR EXCELS

Ramscar was giving one of his best exhibitions of the season. He worked extremely well with Hancocks, whose clever ball control often had the visitors left flank at sixes and sevens.

The snow, another free run moved narrowly and then Bartram flung himself full length to save a rising shot by Forbes.

Shortly before the interval Robinson had a good chance, but he failed to maintain his balance as the ball flashed over from Hurst, and McLean was able to run in and make a timely clearance.

A solo effort by Welsh was well stopped by Galley, and in the last minute of the half Williams made a spectacular save from Hurst.

Half-time:—

WOLVES 2, CHARLTON 0.

Charlton started the second half with two determined raids and Williams had to save in quick succession from Lancelotte and Hurst.

The snow had improved the surface and the players were now standing up to the conditions much better.

Workmen were clearing the touchlines with brooms while play was in progress and Charlton were playing with the snow driving hard in their faces.

NEARLY HEADED INTO OWN GOAL

Wolves were soon away again, and a long dash down the middle saw Westcott shoot just wide with Bartram out of position.

Another grand raid saw Forbes make a lot of ground, but his shot, but well-placed shot was well saved.

In stopping a rising shot from Mullen, Phipps almost headed through his own goal.

Ramscar nearly made it three when, from close range, he hooked the ball up with his left foot, and although Bartram slipped on the ice he managed to get his fingers to it and turn it round the post.

Again the visitors were lucky when Phipps nearly put through his own goal for the second time. Bartram kicked clear from shot was blocked by Ferrier. Half-

B'ham Lose After A Good Start

B IRMINGHAM twice came near to maintain his balance as he was about to try a shot and Phipps cleared with a hefty kick.

Following a free kick taken by Forbes, five yards outside the penalty area, Bartram made another good save, this time from Ramscar.

Wolves' better finishing earned them two more valuable points and there were times when the Charlton defence was very unsteady.

The game provided plenty of good and clean football and of a high standard, taking the conditions into consideration.

Final:—
WOLVES 2, CHARLTON ATH. 0.
Attendance 35,103.

Brentford v. Chelsea

35,000. From the third successive corner kick by Girling, George Smith, Brentford's experimental centre-forward, struck a post, and he continued to cause the Chelsea defence anxiety. Inspired by Macaulay, Brentford attacked strongly, but Chelsea recovered and two Lawton drives brought Crozier full beaten. After 20 minutes PATON gave Chelsea the lead. Half-time:—
Brentford 0, Chelsea 1.

Portsmouth v. Liverpool

30,000. In a snowstorm and on a waterlogged pitch both sides opened strongly. Eastham failed to make the most of a fine chance whilst Barlow narrowly missed with a hard drive. Each side worked hard for a goal, but while Portsmouth were often in the picture by their first real move it was Liverpool's defence was sound. Stubbins passed to Liddell, but his shot was blocked by Ferrier. Half-time—Portsmouth 0, Liverpool 0.

IRMINGHAM twice came quivers of Manchester City in their last 17 games, although scored on a treacherous Maine-road pitch when play began in their game at Manchester today.

MANCHESTER CITY.—McIlvenny, Sproston, Williams; Fagan, McDowall, Emptage; Hawkey, Black, Swift, Westwood.

BIRMINGHAM—Merrick; Jennings, Hughes; Harris, Turner, Mitchell; Mulraney, Dougall, Duckhouse, McIntosh, Edwards.

Swift hurt managed to divert a few yards shot from Mulraney round the post after a defender had slipped heading in the mud.

City played strongly but these positional play was not as good as Birmingham's. Merrick had a quiet time and after Dougall had gone wide with a 30 yards free kick Dsckhouse in the 20th minute saw the ball strike the angle of the upright and crossbar with Swift beaten from a header.

A minute later Merrick had his first real save a header from Swift following a corner kick and then he calmly took a 25 yards pile-driver from Herd at the foot of the post.

Manchester, who were without Wharton, their new winger from Preston, through independence strove hard to get their attack moving smoothly.

Herd was especially prominent but Black headed wide, and then the most part Birmingham's defence find the answer to all their moves. Mulraney was frequently prominent for Birmingham but he was

Croker, of Charlton, had a "shadow" at Molineux today in the shape of a Scottish terrier.

For much of 1946/47, it seemed that Wolves would romp away with their first-ever League Championship. As the grip of one of the worst winters on record relaxed, they found themselves four points clear at the top of the table with at least one game in hand over all their nearest rivals and a 2-0 win over Charlton on 15 March left them with the record of only one defeat in their previous sixteen games.

Then, however, four of the next ten games were lost. Leading scorer Dennis Westcott received a serious injury in a bruising 3-3 draw against Blackburn and Wolves were left to at least draw their last home game against Liverpool on 31 May 1947. The season had been extended to accommodate all the postponements during the winter, at a time when midweek games were not allowed because of possible absenteeism from factories at a desperate time for the country's economy. (Floodlights were of course still a decade in the future.) It is now history that on a blazing hot day in front of a 50,765 gate, Liverpool made the running with Stan Cullis in the last of his 171 games for Wolves twice beaten for pace in the first half by Jack Balmer and Albert Stubbings and though Jimmy Dunn pulled one back for Wolves in the second half, they just couldn't beat former Wolves goalkeeper Cyril Sidlow again.

PRICE — TWOPENCE.

OFFICIAL PROGRAMME

OF

WOLVERHAMPTON WANDERERS FOOTBALL CLUB (1923) LIMITED

MOLINEUX GROUNDS, WOLVERHAMPTON

SEASON 1946-1947

Chairman : J. S. BAKER, Esq.
J. EVANS, Esq.   C. H. HUNTER, Esq.   B. MATTHEWS, Esq.
A. H. OAKLEY, Esq., J.P.
Secretary-Manager : E. T. VIZARD.   Assistant-Secretary : J. T. HOWLEY.
Telephone { 32051/4.   Telegrams : "Wanderers," Wolverhampton.

FOOTBALL LEAGUE (DIVISION I)

LIVERPOOL

v.

WOLVES

at MOLINEUX GROUNDS, WOLVERHAMPTON

SATURDAY, MAY 31st, 1947.

Kick-off 3 p.m.   Match No. 42.

TO-DAY'S SCORE BOARD.

A Arsenal	H W. B. Albion		R
	Man. City		
B Portsmouth	J West Ham		S
Derby County	Burnley		
C Sheffield Utd.	K Walsall		T
Charlton Ath.	Torquay Utd.		
D Chesterfield	L		U
Bury			
E Fulham	M		V
Bradford			
F Luton Town	N		W
Newport C.			
G Nottingham F.	P		X
Plymouth A.	Q		Y

FAULTON BROTHERS, PRINTERS, BERRY STREET, WOLVERHAMPTON.

This autograph sheet brings back memories of Wolves' 1946/47 stalwarts, who came so close to winning the first post-war First Division championship.

Though he has not always had the praise he deserved, manager Ted Vizard (who as a Bolton Wanderers player had played in the first Wembley FA Cup final in 1923) must take a great deal of credit for getting together one of Wolves' greatest-ever sides, signing not only the 'big three' of Jesse Pye, Johnny Hancocks and Bert Williams, but also outstanding supporting cast, such as ball-playing Freddy Ramscar, who went on to give good service to QPR, Preston, Millwall and Northampton.

63

For a time after his retirement as a player, Stan Cullis was officially assistant to Ted Vizard. Wolves finished as high as fifth in the First Division in 1947/48, but in the following summer, Cullis was moved into the manager's chair. In this photograph he is being greeted by skipper Billy Wright with assistant trainer Jack Nelson standing behind Cullis and secretary Jack Howley on the extreme right. The players in this picture include Jimmy Mullen, Alex Simpson, Roy Pritchard, Leslie Smith, Dennis Parsons, Arnold Stephens, Malcolm Clews, Laurie Kelly and Sammy Smyth. Cullis went on to lead Wolves to unprecedented triumphs, and in League games under his management they obtained 792 points from 680 games, won three League Championships and the FA Cup twice, not to mention many notable floodlight friendly games against European opposition. Ted Vizard meanwhile retired from football to keep a hotel in Tettenhall, reflecting that Wolves' record of 103 points from 84 games under his management wasn't so bad either. It is interesting that in the above photograph are Jimmy Mullen, Roy Pritchard, Billy Wright and Sammy Smyth, who were all in the team that brought Stan Cullis the distinction of the FA Cup win in his first season in charge. Jack Nelson is also in the picture; he was a Wolves player in Stan's first season as a player. He went on to play for Luton before the war and later was Walsall first team trainer in the late 1940s and early '50s.

Stan Cullis's first season in charge saw them winning the FA Cup after two unforgettable semi-finals against Manchester United. In the first they held on to draw 1-1 with Manchester United at Hillsborough, despite having both full-backs Roy Pritchard and Laurie Kelly (the latter with a broken ankle) injured in days when no substitutes were allowed. In the replay at Goodison Park a week later, Sammy Smyth followed up his goal in the first game with the matchwinner. Sammy (above) was another Ted Vizard signing, moving from Irish club Dundela in 1947 and going on to score 43 goals in 116 games for Wolves before moving on to Stoke and Liverpool.

A guinea seemed a massive amount to pay for a football game (at a time when one could sit down to watch Wolves at Molineux for four shillings) and a shilling was four times what one normally paid for a match programme, but it was not begrudged by Wolves fans when they saw their side triumph 3-1 in the final over Leiester City.

Billy Wright is chaired off the field with the FA Cup by team-mates Bill Shorthouse and Jesse Pye, with Jimmy Dunn, Bert Williams, Sammy Smyth, Jimmy Dunn and Roy Pritchard also in the picture.

Brothers have figured prominently in Wolves' history. Before the Second World War, as we have seen, Jack and Frank Taylor played together in the defence. Then in the 1949 FA Cup triumph, not only did Billy Crook (left) play in every round, but his brother Alf (right) came in for his first-team debut in the semi-final replay, when both Laurie Kelly and Roy Pritchard were suffering from injuries sustained in the first game. Alf played brilliantly, but in a midweek game at Liverpool four days later he twisted a knee and was never fit for first-team football again – although he did go on to give excellent service to Wellington Town, the forerunners of Telford United. Billy went on to play 221 games for Wolves and he later had a useful spell with Walsall. Both Billy and Alf have in recent years been prominent at ex-Wolves player reunions.

Billy Crook was the perfect example of the local lad who was happy to play literally anywhere for his home-town club. He was just 16 when he made his Wolves debut on the opening day of the 1942/43 season, playing up front and scoring a goal. By the end of wartime football, he had settled into midfield and it was in that position that he made his First Division debut in the first postwar season. He played in one of Wolves' first games against foreign opposition when he scored Wolves' goal in the 1-1 draw against Swedish club Norkopping in November 1947. Later that season, he took over on the left flank of the defence in the Wolves side that missed the First Division Championship by just one point. He then returned to the midfield, where he played in Wolves' 1949 FA Cup winning team.

Jimmy Dunn, who played 144 games and scored 40 goals for Wolves up to 1952, when he left to join Derby County, was the son of a pre-war Scottish international Jimmy Dunn Senior. He also had a brother, Tommy Dunn, who was with Wolves for several seasons after the Second World War without breaking through into the first team. He moved on to give splendid service to Wellington Town in the late 1950s and early '60s.

1953/54 brought Wolves' first-ever First Division championship after a neck-and-neck struggle with West Midland neighbours West Bromwich Albion. Wolves finally clinched the title on the final day of the season with a 2-0 win over Spurs, although Albion did have the consolation of winning the FA Cup with a thrilling 3-2 triumph over Preston at Wembley.

Roy Swinbourne got both goals in that last game of the season against Spurs to take his season's tally to 24, while Johnny Hancocks and Dennis Wilshaw got 25 each. Roy was one of Wolves' finest ever strikers, netting 114 goals in 230 games before his career was tragically ended at the age of twenty-six when he badly injured a knee avoiding cameramen behind the goal in a game at Luton in November 1955.

The 1953/54 season also nearly brought another triumph, as for the second successive season Wolves finished runners-up to Manchester United in the FA Youth Cup, which had just come into existence. Wolves went into this second leg of the final trailing 1-0 from the first, but after a tremendous game that ended 4-4, they had to finally admit defeat. Of that young Wolves side, Gerry Harris, Bobby Mason and Jimmy Murray went on to become first-team regulars, while Geoff Sidebottom and Joe Bonson also had their moments. United's line-up included future manager Wilf McGuiness, first-team regulars David Pegg and Albert Scanlon and two of the game's all-times greats, Bobby Charlton and Duncan Edwards.

Wolves did not win anything in 1954/55, but they finished runners-up to Chelsea in the First Division and their reserves finished third in the Central League. This picture of their professional squad gives some idea of the strength in depth that the club had at that time, as only five of the thirty players pictured did not play in the first team in either that or subsequent seasons. From left to right, back row: George Showell, Gerry Harris, Roy Wickers, Bill Shorthouse, Bert Williams, Ron Flowers, Frank Bolton, Ron Stockin, Eddie Stuart. Third row: Jimmy Murray, Joe Bonson, Bill Guttridge, Noel Dwyer, Nigel Sims, Derek Parton, John Timmins, Roy Pritchard, Bill Slater. Second row: Johnny Hancocks, Peter Broadbent, Roy Swinbourne, Billy Wright, Leslie Smith, Billy Crook. Front row: Noman Deeley, Dennis Wilshaw, Micky Lill, Eddie Clamp, Len Cooper, Tommy McDonald.

At this time Wolves pioneered evening football against Continental opposition – that led in due course to the founding of the European Cup. They took on and beat the best in Europe in a series of floodlit friendlies. Though they had already beaten Maccabi Tel Aviv 10-0, Wolves really took the nation by storm when beating Spartak Moscow 4-0 on 16 November 1954, with all of the goals coming in the second half. Over 55,000 roared Wolves on in their fluorescent shirts as Dennis Wilshaw, Johnny Hancocks (2) and Roy Swinbourne scored the goals.

After the Spartak game, the Wolves directors had been moved to send a letter of congratulation to skipper Billy Wright.

A few weeks later, Wolves did it again: on 13 December 1954 they beat the top Hungarian side Honved 3-2, despite the presence in the Honved side of six of the men who had played in Hungary's recent 6-3 and 7-1 thrashings of the England national team.

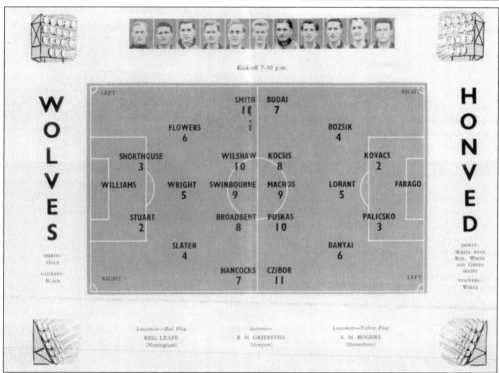

Bill Shorthouse was a stout-hearted Wolves defender who was wounded in the Normandy landings of June 1944, but went on to play in 376 games in Wolves defence. He was not normally expected to leave his defensive duties, but it was he who surged forward to set up the winning goal for Roy Swinbourne in the Honved game. The visitors had led 2-0 at the interval, but then Johnny Hancocks and Roy Swinbourne (with a penalty and a header respectively) brought Wolves back into the game before Roy's unforgettable winner.

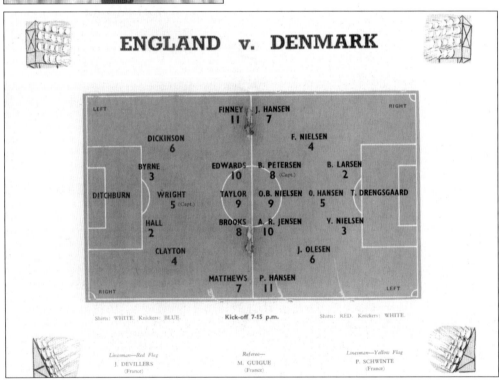

ENGLAND v. DENMARK

LEFT				RIGHT
	FINNEY 11	J. HANSEN 7		
DICKINSON 6			F. NIELSEN 4	
BYRNE 3	EDWARDS 10	B. PETERSEN 8 (Capt.)	B. LARSEN 2	
DITCHBURN	WRIGHT 5 (Capt.)	TAYLOR 9	O.B. NIELSEN 9	O. HANSEN 5	T. DRENGSGAARD
HALL 2	BROOKS 8	A. R. JENSEN 10	V. NIELSEN 3	
CLAYTON 4			J. OLESEN 6	
RIGHT	MATTHEWS 7	P. HANSEN 11		LEFT

Shirts: WHITE. Knickers: BLUE.   Kick-off 7-15 p.m.   Shirts: RED. Knickers: WHITE.

Linesman—Red Flag   Referee—   Linesman—Yellow Flag
J. DEVILLERS   M. GUIGUE   P. SCHWINTE
(France)   (France)   (France)

The success of Wolves' floodlight games continued when in December 1956 they were honoured with the staging of an England v. Denmark World Cup qualifying game, which England won 5-2 with Tommy Taylor (3) and Duncan Edwards (2) getting the goals. The England team was captained by Wolves' very own Billy Wright and the forward line contained both forty-one-year-old Stanley Matthews and twenty-year-old Duncan Edwards. Tragically, three members of the England side, Roger Byrne, Tommy Taylor and Duncan Edwards, died just over a year later in the Munich air disaster, while Jeff Hall died of polio in 1959.

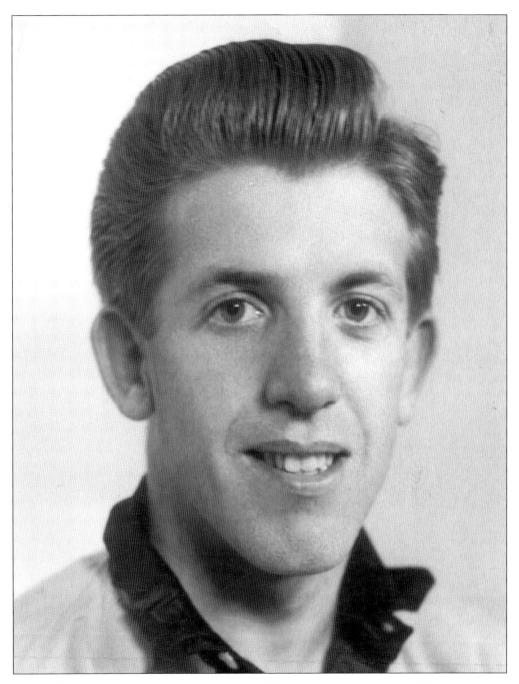

Stan Cullis made relatively few signings during Wolves' glory years of the 1950s, but one that he did make in 1951 was to become an integral part of the great side of the next decade. Peter Broadbent cost just £10,000 when signed from Brentford as a seventeen-year-old in February 1951 and he went on to play 497 games. Though regarded primarily as a skilful ball player, he still managed to score 145 goals, winning three First Division Championship and one FA Cup medal to boot. After leaving Wolves in 1965, he had useful spells with Shrewsbury Town, Aston Villa and Stockport County.

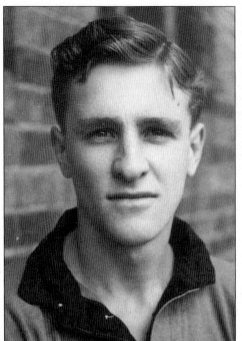

The tremendous amount of talent that was generated by Stan Cullis and his scouting staff in the 1950s meant that many a good player had to move on in order to play regular League football. *Above left:* Eddie Russell played 35 games in midfield before moving to Middlesbrough in 1951. *Above right:* Peter Russell (no relation) played just 4 games in defence before moving to Notts County in 1956 and he was joined there by Eddie a couple of years later. Meanwhile, Bill Guttridge (left) – a native of Darlaston affectionately known as 'Chopper' – moved to Walsall in 1954 after 7 games for Wolves and stayed with the Saddlers until 1962.

Many Wolves players moved to Wellington Town (now Telford United) in the 1950s. When Wolves winger Johnny Hancocks took over at Wellington as player-manager in 1957, he put together a side that regularly contained up to eight ex-Wolves players. This Wellington group consists of, from left to right, back row: Billy Crook, Billy Green, Frank Childs, Dennis Parsons, Alf Crook, Windsor Davies. Front row: Johnny Hancocks, Jack Haines, Ray Pearce, Doug Taylor, Bert Mitchell. Of these players, the two Crooks, Green, Parsons, Davies, Hancocks, Pearce and Taylor were all ex-Wolves players, while Jack Haines was a former West Brom and England man.

Billy Crook, Billy Green and Doug Taylor all went on to play for Walsall and did well for Wolves' Midland neighbours, who were managed by former Wolves boss Major Frank Buckley from 1953 to 1955.

Of the ex-Wolves men who played under Major Buckley at Walsall, by far the most remarkable was Billy Green. He was already established at Fellows Park when Buckley took over there in April 1953, and while he was normally a defender or a midfielder, he had played heroically in goal in a game at Southend on Boxing Day 1951.

For Buckley's first game in charge, Billy played as an emergency striker and scored one of the goals in a 3-0 win over Brighton. In a frequently changing Walsall team, Billy played in every game for three successive seasons before joining Wrexham in 1954. He subsequently played for Wellington, whom he joined in 1957.

1957/58 brought Wolves a second League Championship title, which was achieved with two games to spare.

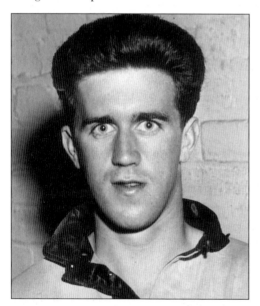

Though Harry Hooper (left) had been Wolves' leading scorer in 1956/57, with 17 goals in his first season after moving from West Ham, he was kept out of the side in 1957/58 by home-grown Norman Deeley. By Christmas, Harry had moved on to Birmingham while Norman, who had been converted from wing-half to become a goalscoring winger, banged home 23 goals. Remarkably, Norman, at just 5ft tall, was even shorter than 5ft 4in Johnny Hancocks who had preceded him in the number 7 shirt up until 1956.

1957/58 was also the season when Wolves topped the Central League, the Birmingham League and the Worcestershire Combination as well as the Football League. To put the lid on things, they also won the FA Youth Cup with a remarkable win over Chelsea in the final. In the first leg at Stamford Bridge, Jimmy Greaves and company seemed to have built up an unassailable 5-1 lead, but in the second leg Wolves roared back to win 6-1.

CHELSEA

Colours—Shirts: Royal Blue (White Collars). Knickers: White. Stockings: Black, Blue and White Tops

1. (Goal)
B. Smart

2. (Right-back)   3. (Left-back)
Shellito   **Legg**

4. (Right-half)   5. (Centre-half)   6. (Left-half)
Dollar BRADBURY   **Scott**   **Long**

7. (Outside-right) 8. (Inside-right) 9. (Centre-forward) 10. (Inside-left) 11. (Outside-left)
Block   **Cliss**   **B. Bridges**   **Greaves**   **Harrison**

Referee:
Mr. L. HOWARTH
(Beverley, Yorks)

Linesmen:
Mr. D. G. JARMIN
(Hemel Hempstead, Herts)
[Red Flag]
Mr. C. R. POULTER
(Hove, Sussex)
[Yellow Flag]

PERRY DURANDT   PAUL HORNE
~~Horne~~ Perry   **Farmer**   **Durandt** ~~Mannion~~
11. (Outside-left) 10. (Inside-left) 9. (Centre-forward) 8. (Inside-right) 7. (Outside-right)

Cocker   **Palin**   **Kirkham**
6. (Left-half)   5. (Centre-half)   4. (Right-half)

Yates   **Kelly**
3. (Left-back)   2. (Right-back)

Cullen
1. (Goal)

WOLVERHAMPTON WANDERERS

Colours—Shirts: Old Gold. Knickers: Black.
Stockings: Old Gold and Black Hoops.

Two members of Wolves' successful FA Youth Cup team. Defender Granville Palin went on to play in Walsall's 1960/61 Third Division promotion team and South African winger Des Horne went on to score 18 goals in 62 first-team games before moving to Blackpool in 1962.

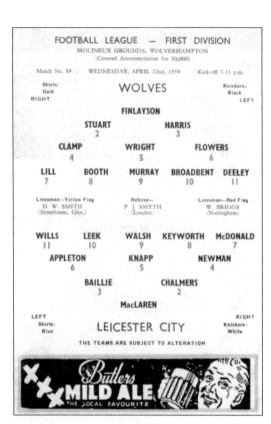

FOOTBALL LEAGUE — FIRST DIVISION

MOLINEUX GROUNDS, WOLVERHAMPTON
(Covered Accommodation for 30,000)

Match No. 39 .. WEDNESDAY, APRIL 22nd, 1959 Kick-off 7-15 p.m.

Shirts:
Gold
RIGHT

WOLVES

Knickers.
Black
LEFT

FINLAYSON

STUART
2

HARRIS
3

CLAMP
4

WRIGHT
5

FLOWERS
6

LILL
7

BOOTH
8

MURRAY
9

BROADBENT
10

DEELEY
11

Linesman—Yellow Flag
D. W. SMITH
(Stonehouse, Glos.)

Referee—
P. J. SMYTH
(London)

Linesman—Red Flag
W. BRIGGS
(Nottingham)

WILLS
11

LEEK
10

WALSH
9

KEYWORTH
8

McDONALD
7

APPLETON
6

KNAPP
5

NEWMAN
4

BAILLIE
3

CHALMERS
2

MacLAREN

LEFT
Shirts:
Blue

LEICESTER CITY

RIGHT
Knickers:
White

THE TEAMS ARE SUBJECT TO ALTERATION

Butlers
XXX MILD ALE
THE LOCAL FAVOURITE

Left: 1958/59 brought a second successive League title to Molineux, this being clinched in a 3-0 win over Leicester in the final home game on 22 April 1959. *Below left*: Jimmy Murray, who had got 29 goals in the previous season, got another 21 and went on to total 166 goals in 299 games before moving to Manchester City in 1963 and then to Walsall in 1966. *Below right*: This was Billy Wright's last season before retirement and, just a week after the championship had been clinched, a civic banquet was held to celebrate the fact that Billy had become the first player to gain 100 England caps. He went on to finish with a total of 105.

COUNTY BOROUGH ⟨crest⟩ OF WOLVERHAMPTON

Civic Banquet

to

Billy Wright

(*Captain of Wolverhampton Wanderers F.C. and England*)

to celebrate his

100 Full Internationals for England

Civic Hall
Wolverhampton

Wednesday
29th April, 1959

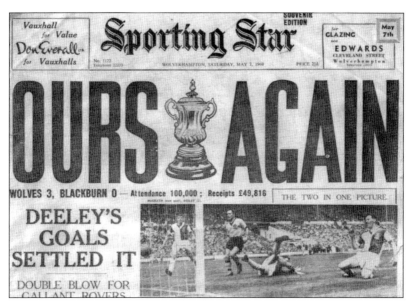

Above: Another Wembley success awaited Wolves in 1960 when they beat Blackburn 3-0. Norman Deeley got two of the goals, but something of the edge was taken off the victory by a serious injury to Rovers defender Dave Whelan early in the game. *Below left*: Bill Slater (pictured with the Footballer of the Year trophy that he won that year) had by this time taken over as Wolves' skipper. He had played as an amateur for Blackpool in the 1951 FA Cup final, joined Wolves in 1952 and played as an amateur for a season and a half before turning professional. All in all, he played 339 games for Wolves and won 12 England caps before moving to Brentford in 1963. *Below right*: The programme for the Cup Final had changed little from 1949, when Wolves had last won the trophy, and still cost one shilling.

One of Wolves' finest-ever midfielders, Ron Flowers shared the glories of the 1950s and the sad decline of the '60s. He made his debut as an eighteen-year-old in a 5-2 defeat by Blackpool in September 1952 and played his last game in a 1-0 defeat at Bristol City in January 1967, when Wolves were striving to climb out of the Second Division. In between, he played in 512 games, scored 37 goals and won three First Division Championship medals, one FA Cup winners' medal and 49 England caps.

Five
Triumphs and Disasters

After just missing out on a Football League and FA Cup double in 1959/60, when pipped in the very last game by Manchester City, Wolves still had a team that looked capable of further glories. Of the players who had appeared in the 1960 FA Cup triumph, George Showell (above left) at twenty-six and Barry Stobart (above right) at twenty-two were still young enough to have many more years before them. Neither quite fulfilled themselves, however, although both had some useful games. After exactly 200 appearance, George moved on to Bristol City in 1965 and later served Wrexham behind the scenes for over ten years. Barry, meanwhile, scored 23 goals in 54 games and then had spells with Manchester City, Aston Villa and Shrewsbury before moving into non-League management with Willenhall and Dudley Town. His sons, Sean and Loy, have also made their mark in local non-League football.

Wolves always seem to have had at least one outstanding goalkeeper on their books and Malcolm Finlayson achieved the virtually impossible feat of making sure that the one and only Bert Williams was not missed when he retired in 1957. Malcolm was twenty-seven at the time and in his first three seasons he helped Wolves to two League Championships and an FA Cup win. In this picture, he peers into the fog during a game at Blackpool in January 1961 that was eventually abandoned. Malcolm went on to make 203 first-team appearances and after success in business he had a short spell as Wolves vice-chairman in 1982.

Bob Wilson is a household name as a former Arsenal goalkeeper and TV presenter, but not everyone knows that he played 4 games in Wolves reserve side in 1961/62 as a twenty-year-old amateur. In this game at Anfield in January 1952 he helped Wolves Reserves to a 1-1 draw against a Liverpool side that included two future first-team stalwarts Tommy Lawrence and Ronny Moran.

After finishing eighteenth in the First Division in 1961/62, Wolves climbed back up to fifth in 1962/63 with two twenty-year-old wingers banging home the goals and thrilling the crowds: Alan Hinton scored 19 and Terry Wharton 16. It seemed that the glory days of the 1950s were returning, with Alan and Terry filling the roles of the legendary Johnny Hancocks and Jimmy Mullen. Alan moved on to Nottingham Forest in 1964, however, and then went on to share in the glory days under Brian Clough at Derby County. Terry moved to Bolton in 1967 after experiencing the agony of relegation and the glory of promotion in his last three seasons with Wolves.

Above: Alan Hinton. *Left*: Terry Wharton.

15 September 1964 was one of the saddest days in the history of Wolves. Stan Cullis, after over thirty years with Wolves as player and manager was sacked despite the fact that on the previous evening Wolves had won a thrilling game 4-3 against West Ham. The whole football world was shocked and while Manchester United manager Matt Busby (in his pre knighthood days) wrote a personal letter of sympathy, Coventry boss Jimmy Hill welcomed Stan to a game at Highfield Road on the following Saturday. Stan went on to manage Birmingham from December 1965 to March 1970, but he never fully recovered from his traumatic sacking. Many of his former players and fans packed into St Peters Church, Wolverhampton for a very moving memorial service to Stan in 2001. The Stan Cullis stand at Molineux is a living monument to this great club servant. Life went on at Molineux, with Wolves losing 2-1 to Blackpool on the following Saturday (as is reported here), while Stan was entertained by Coventry director John Camkin (above).

WOLVES

PERHAPS in this, one of the most vital games in their career, Wolves tried too hard.

It is true Blackpool's forthright opening and two early goals put Wolves at a disadvantage but afterwards it seemed almost as though they could not do right for fear of doing wrong.

In the circumstances, it was significant that one of the few real successes was that old stalwart, George Showell. He did the job in the only way he knew how. For the rest there was far too much inclination to stand off.

Andy Beattie took over as caretaker manager after the departure of Stan Cullis. He had gained an FA Cup winners' medal with Preston North End in 1938 and had won 7 Scotland caps before the war. He was manager of Huddersfield Town when they won promotion from the Second Division in 1953, and also had spells in charge of Barrow, Stockport, Carlisle, Nottingham Forest and Plymouth.

After the departure of Stan Cullis, Wolves actually lost seven games in a row and, despite the efforts of successor Andy Beattie, relegation soon became inevitable. However, Wolves mounted a fine FA Cup run, reaching the last eight and scoring 15 goals in the competition. 53,581 supporters crammed into Molineux for the sixth round tie against Manchester United. Hugh McIlmoyle, who had been bought from Carlisle soon after the departure of Stan Cullis, followed up a fifth round replay hat-trick against Aston Villa with two early goals against United, but Wolves finally went down 5-3.

It seemed that Hugh might be the ideal replacement for Ted Farmer, who had been forced to retire with a knee injury after 44 goals in 62 games and 2 England Under-23 caps. However, Hugh moved on to Bristol City after getting 45 goals in 105 games for Wolves.

Happily, Wolves' stay in the Second Division lasted just two seasons and they roared to promotion in 1966/67, with former Charlton midfielder Mike Bailey (left) taking over as captain.

David Wagstaffe, who had arrived from Manchester City in December 1964, provided inspirational wing play down the left flank. There have been few finer sights in Wolves' history than 'Waggy' in full flight going past man after man.

The return to the First Division in 1967 also brought a change in Wolves' match programme as, after twenty years, the 8-page octavo issue (that had gone up from three old pence to six old pence in two decades) was replaced by a 24-page magazine selling at one shilling. Interestingly enough, both the old style and new style issues reproduced here feature Peter Knowles on the cover.

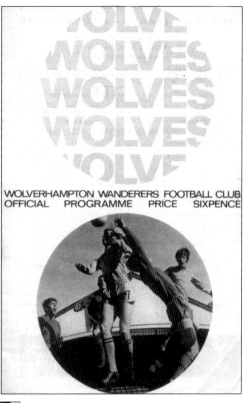

WOLVERHAMPTON WANDERERS FOOTBALL CLUB
OFFICIAL PROGRAMME PRICE SIXPENCE

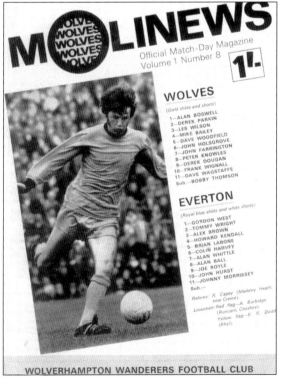

WOLVERHAMPTON WANDERERS FOOTBALL CLUB

Peter Knowles, was a skilful ball player who scored freely but then, after 64 goals in 191 games, retired in 1969 at the age of twenty-four to work for the Jehovah's Witness movement.

Wolves seemed to be on their way back to former glories when they finished as high as fourth in the First Division in 1970/71 with this squad. From left to right, back row: Hugh Curran, Bertie Lutton, John Oldfield, Frank Munro, Phil Parkes, Dave Woodfield, Danny Hegan. Middle row: Les Wilson, Bernard Shaw, Peter Eastoe, Bobby Gould, John Richards, John McAlle, Kenny Hibbitt, Sammy Chung (coach). Front row: Derek Dougan, Dave Wagstaffe, Mike O'Grady, Mike Bailey, Jim McCalliog, Gerry Taylor, Derek Parkin.

Wolves slipped to twelfth in the First Division in 1973/74, but managed to win the Football League Cup with a memorable 2-1 win over Manchester City at Wembley.

THE EMPIRE STADIUM, WEMBLEY

THE FOOTBALL LEAGUE CUP FINAL

SAT., MARCH 2, 1974

KICK-OFF 3.30 p.m.
YOU ARE ADVISED TO TAKE UP
YOUR POSITION BY 3 p.m.

J.S.Lill CHAIRMAN:
WEMBLEY STADIUM LTD

SOUTH STAND SEAT
£3.50

TO BE RETAINED   SEE PLAN AND CONDITIONS ON BACK

TURNSTILES
J or **K**
ENTRANCE
41
ROW
20
SEAT
4

Kenny Hibbitt and John Richards
got the goals and another hero of
the hour was Gary Pierce (right),
who deputised in goal for the
injured Phil Parkes and played
a blinder.

WOLVERHAMPTON WANDERERS

FOOTBALL CLUB (1923) LTD.

Season 1974-75

29

MOLINEUX STREET

CENTRE STAND

0045

Season tickets could still be obtained for as little as £18 in 1974/75. Two men who held season tickets for over fifty years from the 1930s to the '80s were Horace Evans of Essington and Len Mullard of Shareshill. Here they are pictured in the old Molineux Street stand in April 1979. It was demolished soon afterwards, to be replaced by the new John Ireland stand.

The 1970s were great times for durable partnerships, despite Wolves' fluctuating fortunes. John Richards and Derek Dougan regularly played together up front from 1971 to 1974. Derek had joined Wolves from Leicester in 1967 and by the time of his retirement in 1975 had scored 123 goals in 323 games.

John made his debut as a nineteen-year-old in February 1970 and went on to score 195 goals in 488 games before moving to Derby. Derek had a short spell as Wolves chairman in 1982/83, while John served as managing director in the late 1990s.

Frank Munro and John McAlle played together in defence in no fewer than 241 games between 1969 and 1977. Frank came to Wolves from Aberdeen in January 1968, playing 371 games and scored 19 goals before moving to Celtic in December 1977.

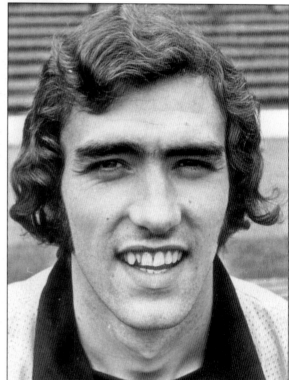

John McAlle was just eighteen when he made his Wolves debut in April 1968 and he played 508 games and scored 3 goals before moving to Sheffield United in 1981.

When Wolves regained their First Division place in 1977, their leading scorers were midfielder Kenny Hibbitt with 17 goals and Alan Sunderland with 16. Kenny was one of Wolves' finest ever signings, moving from Bradford Park Avenue for just £5,000 in November 1968 during Ronnie Allen's brief spell in charge. He figured in both the 1974 and 1980 League Cup wins and was the exemplar of the all-round midfielder – skilful on the ball, with a mastery of the short and long pass, and a tremendous shot. He scored 114 goals in 574 games before moving to Coventry in August 1986. He managed Walsall from 1990 to 1994, Cardiff from 1996/98 and Hednesford in 2001/02.

Alan Sunderland graduated from Wolves junior ranks to play 198 games and score 34 goals before moving to Arsenal in November 1977. At different times he operated successfully in defence, midfield and attack for Wolves, and for Arsenal he scored 92 goals in 290 games, getting the last-minute winner in the 1979 FA Cup final against Manchester United.

Perhaps the least famous of all Wolves' successful managers, Sammy Chung spent just twenty-nine months at the helm from June 1976 to November 1979, but under his inspiration Wolves not only won more games than they lost but also won promotion from the Second Division, reached the last eight of the FA Cup and stayed in the First Division with an unbeaten run of five games at the end of the 1977/78 season. As a player he had been a useful winger with Reading, Norwich and Watford, and after leaving Wolves he had various coaching and assistant manager jobs at home and abroad before returning to management at Tamworth (1991 to 1993) and Doncaster (1994/95).

Above, Sammy is pictured while assistant to Bill McGarmy in 1973/74. From left to right, back row: Derek Jefferson. Kenny Hibbitt, Gerry Taylor, Frank Munro, Derek Dougan, Steve Kindon, Alan Sunderland, Sammy Chung. Middle row: Derek Parkin, Peter Eastoe, Steve Daley, Phil Parkes, Gary Pierce, John McAlle, Geoff Palmer, John Richards. Front row: Jimmy Kelly, Dave Wagstaffe, Barry Powell, Bill McGarry, Mike Bailey, Danny Hegan, Jim McCalliog.

It was on 11 March 1978 that Phil Parkes played the last of his 382 games for Wolves in a career that had begun in the 1966/67 promotion season. 'Lofty', as he was known, went out in a blaze of glory with some brave saves in a 2-1 win at West Ham, playing on after a dislocated finger had been put back into place. He later played football in America.

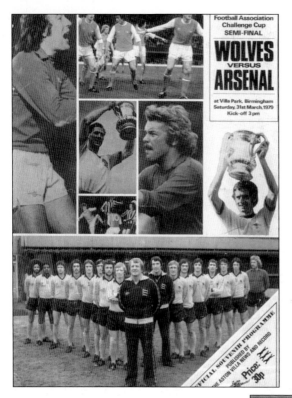

John Barnwell succeeded Sammy Chung in November 1978 and took Wolves to an FA Cup final and a League Cup win within eighteen months of his appointment. Wolves beat Brighton, Newcastle, Crystal Palace and Shrewsbury to earn a semi-final tie against Arsenal in 1979. The first-team squad that took them there lined up as follows, from left to right: George Berry, Bob Hazell, Martin Patching, Geoff Palmer, Mel Eves, John Richards, Peter Daniel, Willie Carr, John Barnwell, Richie Barker, Derek Parkin, Kenny Hibbitt, Wayne Clarke, John McAlle, Billy Rafferty, Colin Brazier and Paul Bradshaw.

Arsenal won the game 2-0 and went on to beat Manchester United 3-2 in the final, with ex-Wolves man Alan Sunderland getting the winning goal. Steve Daley was destined to play only 11 more games for Wolves before his record £1,437,500 transfer to Manchester City. He had played 244 matches for Wolves, but was destined to play only 53 games for City and later played for Burnley and Walsall.

Wolves soon made up for that FA Cup disappointment when they won the Football League Cup in 1980, the second time in seven seasons that they had won this trophy. What's more, it was Peter Shilton of all goalkeepeers who made the mistake that helped Andy Gray to Wolves' winner against Nottingham Forest.

Here, two of the Wembley heroes, Kenny Hibbitt and Peter Daniel, show off the trophy to any of the Molineux faithful who may not have managed to get to Wembley.

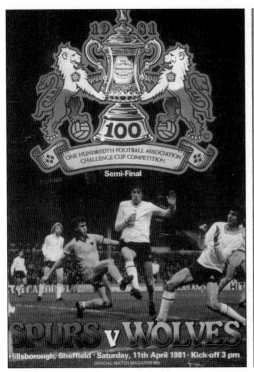

SPURS

1 MILIJA ALEKSIC
2 CHRIS HUGHTON
3 PAUL MILLER
4 GRAHAM ROBERTS
5 STEVE PERRYMAN
6 OSVALDO ARDILES
7 STEVE ARCHIBALD
8 TONY GALVIN
9 GLEN HODDLE
10 GARTH CROOKS
11 GARRY BROOKE
12 GORDON SMITH

WOLVES

PAUL BRADSHAW 1
GEOFF PALMER 2
DEREK PARKIN 3
WAYNE CLARKE 4
JOHN McALLE 5
GEORGE BERRY 6
KENNY HIBBITT 7
WILLIE CARR 8
ANDY GRAY 9
JOHN RICHARDS 10
MEL EVES 11
NORMAN BELL 12

The Men in Charge

REFEREE: Clive Thomas from Porthcawl started refereeing as a teenager after once being on Norwich City's books. Graduated through local and Welsh Leagues to the Football League full list. Has refereed several international and important European matches including two in the 1974 World Cup Finals. During 1976 he was in charge of the FA Cup Final, two international matches – England v Ireland and Germany v Greece – the Bayern Munich v Real Madrid European Cup Semi-Final and the European Nations Cup Final. In 1977 he was in charge of an FA Cup Semi-Final and European Cup matches. In 1978 he officiated in the World Cup in Argentina. Earlier this year he refereed the League Cup Final and the subsequent replay between West Ham United and Liverpool. A married man, with two daughters, he is a group executive, and attends functions as guest speaker, to speak on football refereeing and his other interests include table tennis and basketball.

LINESMEN
Red Flag: D. B. Allison (Lancaster)
Orange Flag: R. F. Nixon (Stockport)

Match Ball:
kindly donated by
Mitre Sports of Huddersfield.

Today's entertainment provided by the:
BAND OF THE IRISH GUARDS
by permission of
Colonel R. T. F. Hume
Lt. Colonel Commanding
Director of Music:
Major M. G. Lane, A.R.C.M. p.s.m.

Pictures:
Wolverhampton Express & Star,
Match Weekly, Sheffield Newspapers,
Tommy Hindley and Steve Ellis.

Magazine Production Team
Designed and Printed by:
J. W. Northend Ltd., Sheffield
Editorial:
Les Comer, Jon Colley and Derek Knight
Colour Plates: Quait Repro, Pinxton, Notts.

Wolves really did seem to be getting back into the big time when, just a year after their League Cup triumph, they not only reached the FA Cup semi-final but took Spurs to a replay, after Willie Carr had converted a last-minute penalty awarded by referee Clive Thomas.

Norman Bell was a substitute in the first leg against Spurs and he then replaced Andy Gray in the second leg. He was one of numerous Wolves strikers whose careers have been curtailed by injury. He really seemed to have arrived when, as a nineteen year old, he got the opening goal in an FA Cup win over Arsenal in January 1975. However, he was never quite the same player after suffering a broken leg in an FA Cup win at Crystal Palace in February 1979. He moved to Blackburn in 1981 after scoring 24 goals in 100 games and again suffered injury.

Twenty-year-old Wayne Clarke was in the Wolves team for the semi-final against Spurs and went on to substitute for Emlyn Hughes in the replay. He was destined to return briefly to Wolves in 1991/92 on loan from Manchester City.

Wayne's elder brother, Derek Clarke, had played 5 games for Wolves in 1969/70 before moving on to Oxford, Leyton Orient and Carlisle.

Wolves lost their First Division place in 1981/82 and fans cast a wistful eye at Peter Withe. He had played 17 games and scored 3 goals for Wolves in 1973, and by 1981 had just helped Aston Villa to the First Division championship and had scored the winner in the final of the 1982 European Cup against Bayern Munich.

Souvenir Brochure

Derek Parkin
TESTIMONIAL YEAR

It was in March 1982 that Derek Parkin played his last game for Wolves, a 3-1 defeat at Villa Park. Derek had come to Wolves from Huddersfield in February 1968 and he set up a new all-time Wolves appearance record of 609. He also scored 10 goals – most of them from the penalty spot, including this one which he fired past Southampton goalkeeper Eric Martin in October 1971.

Briefly, however, it seemed that Wolves might halt the slide as in 1982/83 former defender Graham Hawkins (35 games between 1964 and 1968) celebrated his first season in charge of Wolves by leading them to promotion from the Second Division in 1982/83.

Graham's assistant was Jim Barron, who had played 8 games in goal for Wolves between 1963 and 1965, and had then played for Chelsea, Nottingham Forest, Oxford, Swindon and Peterborough.

Little did the 7,405 fans who attended the Wolves *v*. Leicester game on Monday 7 May 1984 realise that this would be the club's last in the top flight for at least nineteen years. Former Aston Villa and Spurs defender Gordon Smith got the goal that earned Wolves only their sixth win in an unhappy season as, for only the second time in their history (the first was in 1964/65), Wolves lost 25 games in a season. By this time, Jim Barron had taken over from Graham Hawkins as caretaker manager.

DIVISION 1

	P	W	D	L	F	A	W	D	L	F	A	Pts
Liverpool	42	14	5	2	50	12	8	9	4	23	20	88
Southampton	42	15	4	2	44	17	7	7	7	22	21	77
Nottingham F	42	14	4	3	47	17	8	4	9	29	28	74
Manchester U	42	14	3	4	43	18	6	11	4	28	23	74
QPR	42	14	4	3	37	12	8	3	10	30	25	73
Arsenal	42	10	5	6	41	29	8	4	9	33	31	63
Everton	42	9	9	3	21	12	7	5	9	23	30	62
Tottenham H	42	11	4	6	31	24	6	6	9	33	41	61
West Ham U	42	10	4	7	39	24	7	5	9	21	31	60
Aston Villa	42	14	3	4	34	22	3	6	12	25	39	60
Watford	42	9	7	5	36	31	7	2	12	32	46	57
Ipswich T	42	11	4	6	34	23	4	4	13	21	34	53
Sunderland	42	8	9	4	26	18	5	4	12	16	35	52
Norwich C	42	9	8	4	34	20	3	7	11	14	29	51
Leicester C	42	11	5	5	40	30	2	7	12	25	38	51
Luton T	42	7	5	9	30	33	7	4	10	23	33	51
WBA	42	10	4	7	30	25	4	5	12	18	37	51
Stoke C	42	11	4	6	30	23	2	7	12	14	40	50
Coventry C	42	8	5	8	33	33	5	6	10	24	44	50
Birmingham C	42	7	7	7	19	18	5	5	11	20	32	48
Notts Co	42	6	7	8	31	36	4	4	13	19	36	41
Wolves	42	4	8	9	15	28	2	3	16	12	52	29

DIVISION 2

	P	W	D	L	F	A	W	D	L	F	A	Pts
Oxford U	42	18	2	1	62	15	7	7	7	22	21	84
Birmingham C	42	12	6	3	30	15	13	1	7	29	18	82
Manchester C	42	14	4	3	42	16	7	7	7	24	24	74
Portsmouth	42	11	6	4	39	25	9	8	4	30	25	74
Blackburn R	42	14	3	4	38	15	7	7	7	28	26	73
Brighton & HA	42	13	6	2	31	11	7	6	8	23	23	72
Leeds U	42	12	7	2	37	11	7	5	9	29	32	69
Shrewsbury T	42	12	6	3	45	22	6	5	10	21	31	65
Fulham	42	13	3	5	35	26	6	5	10	33	38	65
Grimsby T	42	13	1	7	47	32	5	7	9	25	32	62
Barnsley	42	11	7	3	27	12	3	9	9	15	30	58
Wimbledon	42	9	8	4	40	29	7	2	12	31	46	58
Huddersfield T	42	9	5	7	28	29	6	5	10	24	35	55
Oldham A	42	10	4	7	27	23	5	4	12	22	44	53
Crystal P	42	8	7	6	25	27	4	5	12	21	38	48
Carlisle U	42	8	5	8	27	23	5	3	13	23	44	47
Charlton A	42	8	7	6	34	30	3	5	13	17	33	45
Sheffield U	42	7	6	8	31	28	3	8	10	23	38	44
Middlesbrough	42	6	8	7	22	26	4	2	15	19	31	40
Notts Co	42	6	5	10	25	32	4	2	15	20	41	37
Cardiff C	42	5	3	13	24	42	4	5	12	23	37	35
Wolves	42	5	4	12	18	32	3	5	13	19	47	33

DIVISION 3

	P	W	D	L	F	A	W	D	L	F	A	Pts
Reading	46	16	3	4	39	22	13	4	6	28	29	94
Plymouth A	46	17	3	3	56	20	9	6	8	32	33	87
Derby Co	46	13	7	3	45	20	10	8	5	35	21	84
Wigan A	46	17	4	2	54	17	6	10	7	28	31	83
Gillingham	46	14	5	4	48	17	8	8	7	33	37	79
Walsall	46	15	7	1	59	23	7	2	14	31	41	75
York C	46	16	4	3	49	17	4	7	12	28	41	71
Notts Co	46	12	6	5	42	26	7	8	8	29	34	71
Bristol C	46	14	5	4	43	19	4	9	10	26	41	68
Brentford	46	8	8	7	29	29	10	4	9	29	32	66
Doncaster R	46	7	10	6	20	21	9	6	8	25	31	64
Blackpool	46	11	6	6	38	19	6	6	11	28	36	63
Darlington	46	10	7	6	39	33	5	6	12	22	45	58
Rotherham U	46	13	5	5	44	18	2	7	14	17	41	57
Bournemouth	46	9	6	8	41	31	6	3	14	24	41	54
Bristol R	46	9	8	6	27	21	5	4	14	24	54	54
Chesterfield	46	10	6	7	41	30	3	8	12	20	34	53
Bolton W	46	10	4	9	35	30	5	4	14	19	38	53
Newport Co	46	7	8	8	35	33	4	10	9	17	32	51
Bury	46	11	7	5	46	26	1	6	16	17	41	49
Lincoln C	46	7	9	7	33	34	3	7	13	22	43	46
Cardiff C	46	7	5	11	22	29	5	4	14	31	54	45
Wolves	46	6	6	11	29	47	5	4	14	28	51	43
Swansea C	46	9	6	8	27	27	2	4	17	16	60	43

The speed of Wolves' decline in the mid-1980s is clearly indicated by the League tables. It was little comfort that they picked up four more points in the Second Division than the First and eight more points in the Third Division than the Second.

In the midst of this dramatic decline, two famous managers had spells at the helm, with Tommy Docherty in charge for the Second Division season 1984/85 and Bill McGarry (who in his previous spell from 1968 to 1976 had led Wolves to a League Cup win and a UEFA Cup runners-up spot) going through an unhappy second spell between September and November 1985 as Wolves slipped down the Third Division. Only Bristol City (between 1980 and 1982) had ever before suffered relegation in three successive seasons.

This picture of the 1985/86 Wolves side that unsuccessfully tackled the challenges of Third Division football may bring a reminder of players long forgotten who played a few games. In fact, Wolves used thirty different players in the First Division in 1984/85 and thirty-two in the Second in 1985/86. At various times, both Cavan Chapman and Campbell Chapman, sons of Sammy Chapman who was manager from November 1985 to August 1986, tried their luck in Wolves' front line.

For Wolves' Third Division game against Bolton on 1 February 1986, just 3,110 fans were present. Neither the North Bank terraces nor the Waterloo Road stand was in use and the John Ireland stand was thirty yards from the pitch.

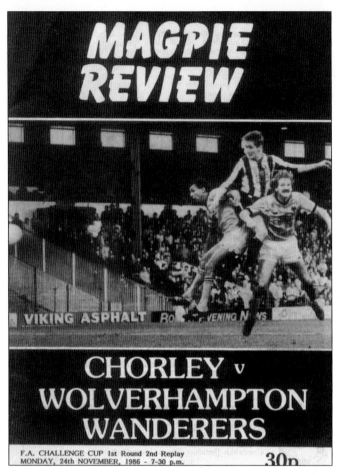

MAGPIE REVIEW

VIKING ASPHALT

CHORLEY v WOLVERHAMPTON WANDERERS

F.A. CHALLENGE CUP 1st Round 2nd Replay
MONDAY, 24th NOVEMBER, 1986 - 7-30 p.m.

30p

These are the teams that participated in the game that saw Wolves at their lowest ebb as they went out of the FA Cup in a second replay of a first round FA Cup tie against a Chorley side who were in the Northern Premier League. Chorley had been drawn at home, but played the game at Bolton's Burnden Park. This ended 1-1, as did the replay at Molineux which went to extra time. Chorley then won the toss for ground advantage and again played at Bolton and won 3-0. Wolves' support was dwindling so much at that time that just 4,790 saw the Molineux game, while 4,887 and 5,421 respectively saw the games at Bolton.

THE MAGPIES   THE WOLVES

Six

The Only Way is Up

Hartlepool 0

Wolves 1

MATCH/ACTION
by Ian Johnson

Bull in charge to lift Wolves

A splendidly taken goal by Steve Bull gave Wolves a well deserved lead at Hartlepool today.

Wolves lost the services of central defender Peter Zelem after 23 minutes with a leg injury but the reshaped side took the lead two minutes later.

A perfect through ball from Jon Purdie sent Bull clear and the former West Bromwich Albion striker rounded keeper Blackburn to slot home a cracker.

HARTLEPOOL: Blackburn, Nobbs, McKinnon, Hogan, Smith, Sword, Dixon, Shoulder, Borthwick, Walker, Lockhart. Sub. Gibb.WOLVES: Barrett, Stoutt, Barnes, Powell, Zelem, Clarke, Purdie, Thompson, Bull, Mutch, Dougherty. Sub. Holmes.Referee Mr. D. Hutchinson (Harrogate).

Wolves forced two quick corners to put Hartlepool under pressure and followed this with a fine shot from Mutch but the effort was just wide of the post.

Powell's experience in midfield instigated the first classy move of the match from which Wolves were close to going ahead.

He combined with Bull, who pulled the ball back across the penalty area but the tacky mud prevented the ball reaching Mutch.

After 15 minutes, central defender Zelem was hurt in a tackle and left limping. He had been Wolves most impressive defender and was switched to the right flank.

Clarke took over at the centre of the Wolves defence and was immediately put under pressure, although Dougherty cleared the danger with a long down-field punt.

The reshaped Wolves side maintained their attacking eagerness and it was Zelem who crossed the ball into the Hartlepool penalty area but Bull's tame header caused no problems.

Hartlepool hit back and Barrett had to dash out of goal to prevent a dangerous move developing into something more serious.

Wolves decided, at this point, that Zelem was not going to recover and he was substituted by Holmes.

Powell, fed by Dougherty, was once again the brains behind the next Wolves attack which gave Mutch a shooting chance but his shot was well saved by goalkeeper Blackburn.

A minute later Wolves deservedly snatched the lead.

A superbly through ball from Purdie split the Hartlepool defence and Bull was sent clear with only the keeper to beat.

He did so and pushed the ball into an empty net.

As soon as the ball went into the net, a large part of the Hartlepool crowd ran onto the pitch and taunted the 50 or 60 Wolves fans behind the goal.

A nasty incident looked likely but a larger police force than normal kept the fans apart.

Wolves were driving hard to win possession at every opportunity and it was this type of aggression from Bull which gave Mutch another half chance.

The striker hammered the ball on the turn but the heavy mud helped to make it an easy save for Blackburn.

With 35 minutes gone, a slick move was started by Barnes with a throw-in to Bull and his snappy centre was hit first time by Dougherty but his shot, on the volley, went over the bar.

Hartlepool tried to force their way back into the game and a free kick from Hogan was just touched wide for a corner by Barrett.

But with half time approaching, Wolves were caught flat-footed when a shot on the turn from Shoulder beat Barrett but just shaved the far post.

Half-time:
Hartlepool.................. 0
Wolves........................ 1

The heavy pitch was causing problems early in the second half and two badly timed back passes almost had Wolves in trouble.

The second one, from Stoutt, had to be hacked clear by Barrett who had raced out of his own penalty area.

At the other end, Mutch ran into the same problem when trying to find Dougherty with a low cross.

Wolves were continuing to be enterprising and Powell drilled a low ball for Dougherty to run on to and his low cross was met first time by Mutch.

Under pressure from Smith, he hit the ball, first time, high and wide.

Hartlepool were, however, game and almost hit back 10 minutes into the second half when a Lockhart header just missed the far post with Barrett stranded.

Wolves went close to increasing their lead when a throw-in from Thompson put Mutch in possession. He went round a Hartlepool defender to drill in a low cross which Purdie was just inches away from pushing into the net.

Wolves couldn't afford to be complacent and almost conceded their lead in the 62nd minute.

A chip from Lockhart put Shoulder clear. He went round Barrett and with the net empty, his shot hit the post and rebounded for Stoutt to gratefully concede a corner.

A minute later, it was Thompson's turn to clear the ball off the line with the Wolves defence, all of a

Franke's in front

West Germany's Franke Sloothaak won the World Cup qualifying round at the Olympia International Showjumping Championships this afternoon.

The 28-year-old pupil of Paul Schockemohle beat four other riders in the second, timed jump-off, riding his 16-year-old brown gelding, Farmer.

Schockemohle himself finished enough points to regain the European League lead he lost to France's Pierre Durand in Bordeaux last week.

Ireland's Eddie Macken finished second and is now also second in the League. His mount was Carrolls Piquet, whom he has ridden for just three weeks.

Sloothaak is now fourth in the League with Peter Charles the high-

Wolves' motto 'Out of Darkness Cometh Light' was never more true than in November 1986, for just days before that Chorley FA Cup debacle, a certain Stephen George Bull was signed from West Bromwich Albion, together with an Andrew Richard Thompson, as the then manager of Wolves' West Midland rivals strove to slim down his playing staff. While Andy settled first into midfield and then into defence, Steve opened his account in a Freight Rover Trophy game at Cardiff and then in his second League match got the winner at Hartlepool on 13 December 1986.

This really was the start of something big as Steve Bull (right) linked up with Andy Mutch (left), who had joined Wolves from Southport in February 1986 during Sammy Chapman's time in charge. Andy had scored 12 goals by the time Steve arrived, but they were destined to become one of the finest dual spearheads Wolves have ever fielded. As they got into gear so did Wolves, and by the time Andy moved to Swindon in August 1993 he had scored 105 goals in 338 games while Steve went on to score an amazing 306 goals in 559 games before injury cruelly ended his career in 1999. Though he was playing in the Third Division at the time, Steve scored against Scotland in the first of his 13 England appearances and was awarded the MBE in the Queen's Millennium New Year's honours list.

1987-88

Manager: Graham Turner

#		Date	Venue/Opponent	Result	Scorers	Att.
1	Aug	15 (a)	Scarborough	D 2-2	Bull, Stoutt	7,314
2		22 (h)	Halifax T	L 0-1		7,223
3		29 (a)	Hereford U	W 2-1	Bull, Mutch	2,628
4		31 (h)	Scunthorpe U	W 4-1	Bull 2, Mutch 2	6,672
5	Sep	5 (a)	Cardiff C	L 2-3	Bull, Vaughan	2,256
6		12 (h)	Crewe A	D 2-2	Bull, Gallagher	8,285
7		16 (a)	Peterboro' U	D 1-1	Bull	3,089
8		19 (a)	Stockport C	W 2-0	Mutch, Robinson	2,233
9		26 (h)	Torquay U	L 1-2	Bull	7,349
10		29 (h)	Rochdale	W 2-0	Bull, Mutch	5,553
11	Oct	3 (a)	Bolton W	L 0-1		3,803
12		10 (a)	Carlisle U	W 1-0	Bull	2,620
13		17 (h)	Tranmere R	W 3-0	Bull, Mutch, Vaughan	6,608
14		20 (h)	Cambridge U	W 3-0	Bull, Mutch, Vaughan	6,492
15		24 (a)	Darlington	D 2-2	Mutch 2	2,282
16		31 (h)	Newport C	W 2-1	Mutch, Vaughan	6,467
17	Nov	3 (a)	Swansea C	W 2-1	Bull, Gallagher	5,293
18		7 (h)	Burnley	W 3-0	Downing, Gallagher, Vaughan	10,002
19		21 (a)	Colchester U	W 1-0	Thompson	2,413
20		28 (h)	Wrexham	L 0-2		8,541
21	Dec	12 (a)	Hartlepool U	D 0-0		2,760
22		19 (h)	Leyton O	W 2-0	Bull 2	12,051
23		28 (h)	Exeter C	W 3-0	Dennison, Mutch, Thompson	15,588
24	Jan	1 (h)	Hereford U	W 2-0	Bull 2	14,577
25		2 (a)	Crewe A	W 2-0	Mutch 2	4,629
26		16 (h)	Stockport C	D 1-1	Vaughan	8,672
27		30 (a)	Scunthorpe U	W 1-0	Mutch	5,476
28	Feb	6 (h)	Cardiff C	L 1-4	Bull	9,077
29		13 (a)	Exeter C	W 4-2	Bull 3, Purdie	3,483
30		16 (h)	Halifax T	L 1-2	Bellamy	2,281
31		19 (h)	Scarborough	D 0-0		11,391
32		23 (a)	Torquay U	D 0-0		3,805
33		27 (h)	Bolton W	W 4-0	Bull 2, Dennison, Robinson	12,430
34	Mar	1 (h)	Rochdale	W 1-0	Holmes	2,805
35		4 (a)	Tranmere R	W 3-1	Bellamy, Mutch, Clark (og)	5,007
36		12 (a)	Carlisle U	L 0-3		9,262
37		22 (h)	Peterboro' U	L 0-1		8,049
38		26 (h)	Darlington	W 5-3	Bull 3, Chard, Robinson	9,349
39	Apr	2 (a)	Burnley	W 3-0	Bull, Holmes, Mutch	10,341
40		4 (h)	Colchester U	W 2-0	Bull 2	13,442
41		10 (a)	Cambridge U	D 1-1	Mutch	5,107
42		23 (h)	Swansea C	W 2-0	Bull, Robinson	12,344
43		26 (a)	Newport C	W 3-1	Bull 2, Mutch	3,409
44		30 (a)	Wrexham	L 2-4	Chard, Mutch	8,698
45	May	2 (h)	Hartlepool U	W 2-0	Bull 2	17,895
		7 (a)	Leyton O	W 2-0	Dennison, Robinson	7,738

An idea of just how Steve Bull (supported by Andy Mutch) monopolised Wolves' goalscoring in 1987/88 may be gauged from this list of results. In just 8 Sherpa Van games, Steve got 12 goals – and yet it was Andy Mutch and Robbie Dennison who netted in the final.

108

DIVISION 4											
	P	W	D	L	F	A	W	D	L	F	A Pts
Wolves	46	15	3	5	47	19	12	6	5	35	24 90
Cardiff C	46	15	5	2	39	14	9	7	7	27	27 85
Bolton W	46	16	5	2	42	12	7	6	10	24	30 78
Scunthorpe U	46	14	5	4	42	20	6	12	5	34	31 77
Torquay U	46	10	7	6	34	16	11	7	5	32	25 77
Swansea C	46	9	7	7	35	28	11	3	9	27	28 70
Peterboro' U	46	10	5	8	28	26	10	5	8	24	27 70
Leyton Orient	46	13	4	6	55	27	6	8	9	30	36 69
Colchester U	46	10	5	8	23	22	9	5	9	24	29 67
Burnley	46	12	5	6	31	22	8	2	13	26	40 67
Wrexham	46	13	3	7	46	26	7	3	13	23	32 66
Scarborough	46	12	8	3	38	19	5	6	12	18	29 65
Darlington	46	13	6	4	39	25	5	5	13	32	44 65
Tranmere R*	46	14	2	7	43	20	5	7	11	18	33 64
Cambridge U	46	10	6	7	32	24	6	7	10	18	28 61
Hartlepool U	46	9	7	7	25	26	6	7	10	25	32 59
Crewe A	46	7	11	5	25	19	6	8	9	32	34 58
Halifax T†	46	14	2	7	43	20	5	7	13	17	34 55
Hereford U	46	8	7	8	25	27	6	5	12	16	32 54
Stockport Co	46	7	7	9	26	26	5	8	10	18	32 51
Rochdale	46	5	9	9	28	34	6	6	11	19	42 48
Exeter C	46	8	6	9	33	29	3	7	13	20	39 46
Carlisle U	46	9	5	9	38	33	3	3	17	19	53 44
Newport C	46	4	5	14	19	36	2	2	19	16	69 25

DIVISION 3											
	P	W	D	L	F	A	W	D	L	F	A Pts
Wolves	46	18	4	1	61	19	8	10	5	35	30 92
Sheffield U	46	16	3	4	57	21	9	6	8	36	33 84
Port Vale	46	15	3	5	46	21	9	5	9	32	27 84
Fulham	46	12	7	4	42	28	10	2	11	27	39 75
Bristol R	46	9	11	3	34	21	10	6	7	33	30 74
Preston NE	46	14	7	2	56	31	5	8	10	23	29 72
Brentford	46	14	5	4	36	21	4	9	10	30	40 68
Chester C	46	12	6	5	38	18	7	5	11	26	43 68
Notts Co	46	11	7	5	37	22	7	6	10	27	32 67
Bolton W	46	12	8	3	42	23	4	8	11	16	31 64
Bristol C	46	10	3	10	32	25	8	6	9	21	30 63
Swansea C	46	11	8	4	33	22	4	8	11	18	31 61
Bury	46	11	7	5	27	22	5	6	12	28	45 61
Huddersfield T	46	10	8	5	35	25	7	1	15	28	48 60
Mansfield T	46	10	8	5	32	22	4	9	10	16	30 59
Cardiff C	46	10	9	4	30	16	4	6	13	14	40 57
Wigan A	46	9	5	9	28	22	5	9	9	27	31 56
Reading	46	10	6	7	37	29	5	5	13	31	43 56
Blackpool	46	10	6	7	36	29	4	7	12	20	30 55
Northampton T	46	11	2	10	41	34	5	4	14	23	49 54
Southend U	46	10	9	4	33	26	3	6	14	23	49 54
Chesterfield	46	9	5	9	35	35	5	2	16	16	51 49
Gillingham	46	7	3	13	25	32	5	1	17	22	49 40
Aldershot	46	7	6	10	29	29	1	7	15	19	49 37

DIVISION 2											
	P	W	D	L	F	A	W	D	L	F	A Pts
Leeds U	46	16	6	1	46	18	8	7	8	33	34 85
Sheffield U	46	14	5	4	43	27	10	8	5	35	31 85
Newcastle U	46	17	4	2	51	26	5	10	8	29	29 80
Swindon T	46	12	6	5	49	29	8	8	7	30	30 74
Blackburn R	46	10	9	4	43	30	9	8	6	31	29 74
Sunderland	46	10	8	5	41	32	10	6	7	29	32 74
West Ham U	46	14	5	4	50	22	6	7	10	30	35 72
Oldham A	46	15	7	1	50	23	4	7	12	20	34 71
Ipswich T	46	13	7	3	38	22	6	5	12	29	44 69
Wolves	46	12	5	6	37	20	6	8	9	30	40 67
Port Vale	46	11	9	3	37	20	4	7	12	25	37 61
Portsmouth	46	9	8	6	40	34	6	8	9	22	31 61
Leicester C	46	10	8	5	34	29	5	6	12	33	50 59
Hull C	46	7	8	8	27	31	7	8	8	31	34 58
Watford	46	11	6	6	41	28	3	9	11	17	32 57
Plymouth A	46	8	6	9	30	23	5	5	13	28	40 55
Oxford U	46	8	7	8	35	31	7	2	14	22	35 54
Brighton & HA	46	8	7	8	27	28	7	3	15	28	45 54
Barnsley	46	7	9	7	22	23	6	6	11	27	48 54
WBA	46	9	9	5	37	27	5	3	15	20	45 53
Middlesbrough	46	10	3	10	33	29	3	8	12	19	34 50
Bournemouth	46	8	6	9	30	31	4	6	13	27	49 49
Bradford C	46	9	6	8	26	24	0	8	15	18	44 41
Stoke C	46	4	11	8	20	24	2	8	13	15	39 37

There was some disappointment when Wolves missed out in the Fourth Division play-off final of 1986/87, going down 3-0 on aggregate to an Aldershot side who were destined to drop out of the Football League just four seasons later. However, there was no stopping Wolves over the next two seasons as they topped the Fourth Division with 90 points and 82 goals in 1987/88 and did even better a season later in the Third with 92 points and 96 goals.

Wolves' 1987/88 Fourth Division championship season began with a 2-2 draw at Scarborough in what was the home side's first ever Football League game. 7,314 saw the match and this still stands as a record League attendance for the Yorkshire club, who lost their Football League place in 1999.

1988 also brought Wolves a Wembley success when they beat Burnley 2-0 in the final of the Sherpa Van Trophy. A record gate for the competition of 80,841 turned out for this game between two former First Division rivals and the scene that welcomed the victorious Wolves back to Wolverhampton could well have been mistaken for that of welcoming FA Cup winners.

PROFILE
Robbie Dennison

I'll never forget that very special moment

One of the Wembley heroes was Robbie Dennison, who had joined Wolves from West Brom just four months after Andy Thompson and Steve Bull had made the same journey. His magnificent goal from a freekick to put Wolves 2-0 up was the highest moment in a Wolves career that lasted until 1997 and in which he scored 49 goals in 453 games.

Wolves' two season spell in the Fourth Division brought them into contact again with teams that they had not met for many years. The games with Rochdale brought back memories of the 1923/24 season, when Wolves pipped their Lancashire rivals for top place.

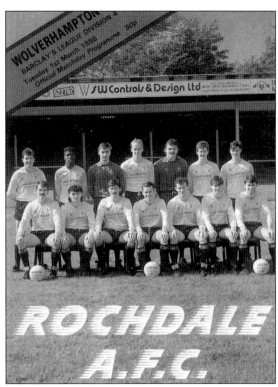

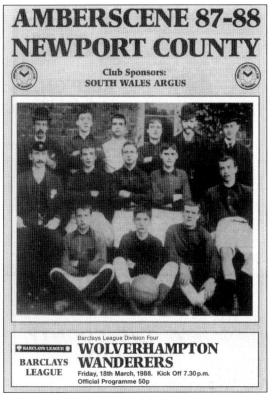

The games with Newport recalled wartime battles with the Welsh club, and it is sad to reflect that when Wolves played at Somerton Park on 18 March 1988, the home side were destined to play only five more games there before losing their Football League place and shortly afterwards going out of existence for a spell. Happily, they are now re-formed and are playing in the Premier Division of the Dr Martens League.

This is the 'dream team' of manager Graham Turner and chief scout Ron Jukes, who somehow got together a team that took Wolves from the Fourth Division to the top half of the Second Division between 1987 and 1990. Graham was an outstanding defender with Wrexham, Chester and Shrewsbury, before becoming player-manager of the Shrews in 1978. In six years in charge, he took Shrewsbury up to the Second Division for the first time in their history and also to a sixth round FA Cup tie against Wolves in 1980. He managed Aston Villa from 1984 to 1986 and then took over Wolves in October 1986 after Brian Little had made a useful start to the season as caretaker. A month after Graham's appointment came the Chorley FA Cup debacle. A fortnight after that he took on Ron Jukes as chief scout. Ron had enjoyed two highly successful spells with Walsall, discovering future internationals Allan Clarke and Phil Parkes amongst many others, and had worked successfully with Graham at Shrewsbury. During their partnership at Wolves, which lasted until 1994, Wolves topped the Fourth Division and the Third Division in successive seasons and finished successively tenth, twelfth, eleventh, eleventh and eighth in the Second Division (that was relabelled Division One in 1992).

As Wolves got into their goalscoring stride in the late 1980s, the free-scoring front line brought back memories of the 1950s. There were also some old scores that were settled. When Wolves beat Mansfield 6-2 for instance, just before Christmas 1988, there were those amongst the 12,134 gate who had been at Molineux on 12 January 1929 when Mansfield – who had not then achieved Football League status – beat Wolves 1-0 in an FA Cup tie in front of 21,837 fans. The goals in this 1988 games were scored by Steve Bull (3), Mick Gooding, Andy Mutch and Andy Thompson.

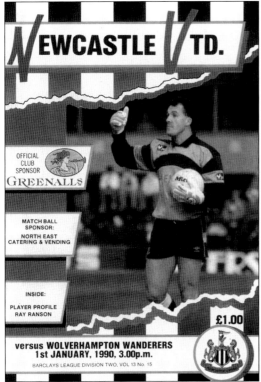

Happily, the goalscoring habit carried over into the Second Division, and on New Year's Day 1990 Wolves achieved a remarkable 4-0 win at St James's Park, Newcastle. Steve Bull, in one of his finest-ever games for Wolves (and that's saying something), got all four goals. Another remarkable feature of the game was that a specially chartered flight carried a group of Wolves fans to the game, in the Newcastle goal was former Wolves favourite John Burridge and up front was future Wolves manager Mark McGhee.

Wolves met Leicester in the Second Division on 10 April 1990. Leicester were the team against whom Wolves had chalked up a record 10-1 win in April 1937 and whom Wolves had beaten 3-1 in the 1949 FA Cup final. Results had not always gone Wolves' way in between, but Steve Bull and Robbie Dennison did their stuff again as they shared the goals in a 5-0 win, Bully getting a hat-trick. On the front cover of the programme that night was Wolves' tough-tackling midfielder Keith Downing, who went on to play 228 games and score 11 goals before moving on to rejoin manager Graham Turner at Hereford. He returned to Molineux as youth team coach in March 1999.

Wolves' first four seasons back in the Second Division, were what might be called a model of consistency. Although results were constant, the ground development was meteoric as a new Molineux arose and, after suffering the agony of a stadium that at one stage was closed on two of the four sides, it was a delight to see the opening of a new ground that was celebrated with a game against Kispest Honved of Hungary in December 1993.

A celebration of the completion of

THE NEW Molineux Stadium

Tuesday 7th December, 1993

• featuring •

a special commemorative match

WOLVES ✦ **Kispest Honved** (Hungary)

Kick Off 7.45pm

special souvenir brochure ✦ £2.00

The stars come out for Billy Wright

...tars shone for Billy Wright at Molineux last night — joining in ebrations at the official opening of the £5m Billy Wright Stand. f Billy's former Wolves and England team-mates helped him he night with a touch of nostalgia, and then, donning his ' director's cap, the latest Wolves team marked it with three It was a great opportunity to again salute the heroes of the lineux days — no doubt some of them stunned by the new-look — the players who remember the Cow Shed, the South Bank, lineux Street and Waterloo Road stands. And four who had no m recalling those days are (below) Bobby Charlton, Eddie Clamp, Billy Crook and Bryan Douglas.

■ The Molineux greats, the England men . . . they were help William Ambrose Wright, CBE, 105 caps for Englan another moment of footballing glory. Below are (le Norman Deeley, Ronnie Clayton, Peter Broadbent and the Cullis. Alongside them ranged the likes of Bert Willia Hancocks, Malcolm Finlayson, Bill Slater, Bill Shorthouse bourne and Don Howe. And it was a family occasion, to wife Joy and her sisters marked the occasion with a Beve rendition of Happy Wanderer. Altogether, a night oldies . . .

Just a few months earlier, the Billy Wright stand had been opened and Billy himself was there, together with numerous former players, to see Wolves beat Millwall 2-0.

Sadly, just a year after the opening of the Billy Wright stand, Billy died at the age of seventy.

This is one of the last pictures of Billy, singing along with the legendary Beverley sisters, who comprised his wife Joy (centre) and twin sisters Teddy and Babs. How bravely Joy conducted herself at the very moving funeral service on Monday 12 September 1994. Not only was St Peters church full, but the service was relayed to hundreds of fans who stood in the rain outside and joined in the singing of 'Onward Christian Soldiers' and (of course) 'The Happy Wanderer'.

Wolves' dreams of a return to the big time are just three tantalising games away. The slumbering Black Country giants are the nearest yet to bringing back Molineux's golden days.

But even their loyalist fans realise the team Graham Taylor has brought at a cost of £6 million could slip up in the play-offs.

The first crunch comes tomorrow with a mammoth semi-final first-leg against Bruce Rioch's Bolton Wanderers followed by the return at Burnden Park on Wednesday.

But it does not end there. Victory over Bolton has to be followed by a Wembley triumph over Tranmere or Reading at Wembley on May 29.

Only then can they take their place in the FA Premiership with the prestige and financial rewards that will bring.

It's certainly the biggest challenge Taylor has ever faced. Bigger even than when he was charged with the task of taking England to the World Cup finals in the United States.

That failure saw him disgracefully labelled as a "turnip head". Sadly, it will stay with him for the rest of his life.

But now Taylor has a glorious opportunity to erase some of those horrendous England memories. Taking Wolves to the Premier League would ease the pain.

Whether it will ever disappear entirely from his record is extremely dubious and

by IAN WILLARS
(Sports Argus chief soccer writer)

● Graham Taylor

Taylor can't afford to fail

debatable.

The great expectancy at Wolves has remained with them from the start of the season especially after owner and president Sir Jack Hayward opened his cheque book to the tune of £25 million.

That was what it cost to refurbish Molineux into a great stadium and buy in former Villa wingers Tony Daley and Steve Froggatt for £2.5 million plus Neil Emblen from Millwall for another £1 million.

The massive spending spree didn't stop there, either. Don Goodman was engaged for £1 million. Dutch international John de Wolf arrived from Feyenoord for £600,000, Dean Richards was secured from Bradford on

loan with the promise of another £1 million fee with influential ex-England midfielder Gordon Cowans recruited for a mere £20,000 from Derby County.

Ironically, old hand Cowans, a vastly experienced campaigner from Villa, Blackburn Rovers and Derby, could yet hold the key to their promotion fate.

But, tragically, Wolves have lost all their big money purchases through injury. Daley, Froggatt, de Wolf, Neil Emblen and former skipper Geoff Thomas fell victims of an incredible injury curse and will not be available until next season.

Wolves run-in, like their play-off rivals, has been anything but convincing. Unbeaten in their last five games they have been - but four have been drawn.

The creaky defence has been sorted out. But now they have to emerge victorious against Bolton if they are to reach the final pinnacle at Wembley.

My forecast? A narrow 1-0 win over Bolton tomorrow and a draw at Burnden on Wednesday. If they can achieve that I'll take them to triumph at Wembley where they'll be backed by at least 50,000 devoted fans.

WOLVES: Stowell, Thompson, Venus, Rankine, Richards, Shirtliff, Goodman, Kelly, Bull, Cowans, Dennison. Subs: Wright, Smith, Jones.

Graham Taylor was not universally popular during the 1994/95 season when he was in charge of Wolves, but there is no disputing the fact that he took Wolves into the play-offs and the above article leaves one wondering just what would have happened if Wolves had won through in that controversial semi-final against Bolton. The mid-1990s brought mixed fortunes for Wolves as, sandwiched between two play-off appearances in 1995 and 1997, there was a relegation scare in 1995/96 when Wolves ended up in twentieth spot. The mid-1990s also brought sad news of the deaths of two former Wolves stalwarts, Jack Dowen and Eddie Clamp.

Jack Dowen played for Wolves between 1934 and 1938, with a brief spell at West Ham punctuating his 12 games for Wolves as a no-nonsense defender known affectionately as 'Chopper'. He also played in 61 wartime games while guesting from Hull City. After the war he returned to Wolves and filled a variety of roles as he completed fifty years with the club. At various times he was first-team trainer, coach, scout, kitman and he also shared caretaker manager duties with Gerry Summers for the 5-0 win against Newcastle in November 1968, just before the arrival of Bill McGarry.

Eddie Clamp was one of four England international midfielders on Wolves' books in 1957/58, the others being Billy Wright, Bill Slater and Ron Flowers. Eddie made his first team debut as a nineteen-year-old in a 1-0 defeat at Old Trafford in March 1954 and went on to play 241 games and score 25 games before moving to Arsenal in 1961. Later, he played for Stoke, Peterborough, Worcester and Lower Gornal, and for many years afterwards played in charity games. His mother was also well known at Molineux as a laundry lady.

Neil Emblen is one of relatively few players over the years who have had two separate spells with Wolves. A splendidly versatile player, who at various times figured in midfield, defence and up front, Neil joined Wolves from Millwall in July 1994. He played 104 games and scored 10 goals, and then moved to Crystal Palace in August 1997. He returned to Wolves in March 1998, played another 45 games and struck another 2 goals. He moved to Norwich in July 2001.

One of the happiest aspects of Wolves' prolonged spell in the Second Division (that became Division One) which lasted throughout the 1990s and beyond has been that the club tradition for discovering home-grown talent has been maintained. Lee Naylor (left) was just seventeen when he made his first-team debut against Birmingham in October 1997. On his day a formidable wing back, he had played 164 games by the summer of 2002 and had scored 4 goals, besides winning 2 England Under-21 caps. Carl Robinson (right) played in an Auto Windscreens final while on loan to Shrewsbury before making his Wolves debut as a twenty year old against Norwich in April 1997. By the time he moved on in the summer of 2002, he had played in 184 games in midfield and had scored 2 goals. He also won the man of the match award on his debut for Wales against the Ukraine in March 2001.

Every now and then a star is born and it happened on 9 August 1997 when Robbie Keane, aged 17 years and 2 days, made his League debut for Wolves in the opening game of the new season against Norwich and scored two goals. Rarely has a seventeen-year-old shown such maturity, and this picture from Robbie's first season shows him confidently directing operations. Robbie scored again in the return game against Norwich in the following January, en route to 11 goals in 4 games in that first season. Robbie went on to score 27 goals in 83 games for Wolves before moving to Coventry in August 1999. He seemed to be a bargain at £6 million, the highest fee ever received by Wolves. He has since played for Inter Milan and Leeds, and has been a key figure in the Republic of Ireland team, scoring an unforgettable last-minute equaliser against Germany in the 2002 World Cup. Ironically, Dougie Freedman, who got a hat-trick in this second Norwich game, moved on to Nottingham Forest just seven months later. After having much the better of games against Norwich over the years, Wolves went down to them in the 2002 play-offs.

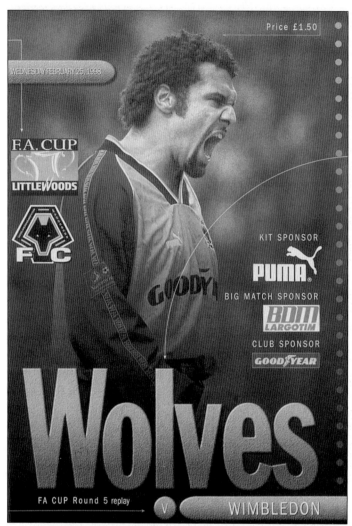

1997/98 also brought a cheering FA Cup run. There was a time when a game against Wimbledon would have left Wolves in danger of becoming victims of a giantkilling, but it was Wolves who embarrassed a side from a higher division on this occasion, beating the Premiership Dons on 25 February 1998 in a fifth round replay. Carl Robinson and Dougie Freedman got Wolves' goals, after Vinnie Jones had given the Dons the lead in what was his last game but two before moving to Queens Park Rangers. Wolves then went on to beat Leeds 1-0, before losing 1-0 to Arsenal in the semi-final.

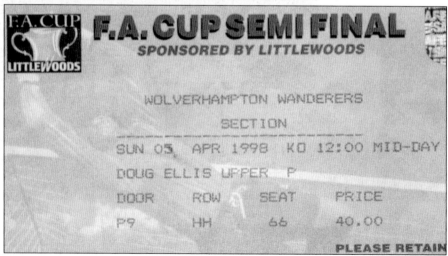

122

YOUTH
Wolves

MIDLAND YOUTH LEAGUE CUP FINAL   V   NOTTS COUNTY YOUTH

1997/98 was also a good season for Wolves youths, who did the double, winning the Midland Melville League and beating Notts County 2-0 in the final of the Midland League Youth Cup, Joleon Lescott and Mark Jones getting the goals.

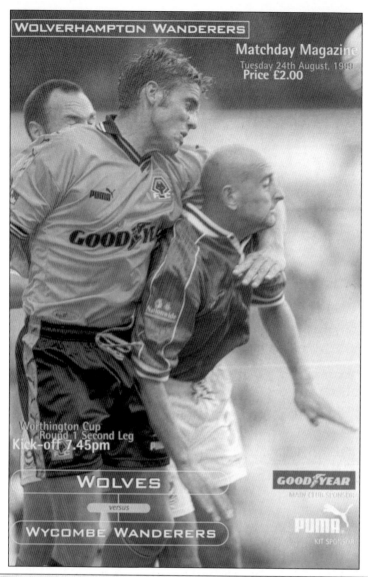

WOLVERHAMPTON WANDERERS

Matchday Magazine
Tuesday 24th August, 1999
Price £2.00

Worthington Cup
Round 1 Second Leg
Kick-off 7.45pm

WOLVES

versus

WYCOMBE WANDERERS

GOOD YEAR
MAIN CLUB SPONSOR

PUMA
KIT SPONSOR

1998/99 saw Wolves just missing out on the play-offs, but if that was a disappointment, what about the one in the following August when Wolves won the away leg of a first round Worthington Cup game with Wycombe but then crashed out 4-2 in the replay at Molineux? None of the 13,723 present that night will ever forget the name of Jermaine McSporran, who got two of the visitors' goals.

efeat has Wolves fans embittered at Keane afterma

ED SCOTT
Birmingham Post

t a week ago, Robbie Keane was Wolverhampton Wanderers player all was relatively right with the neux world.

t night, it was Wolves themselves didn't know whether they were ig or going.

was embarrassment enough to e the Worthington Cup on home Division Two opposition for the d year running — by double the n which Bournemouth managed eptember.

the fans' anger at the transfer- t inactivity in the six days since e's £6 million departure to Coven- ity was last night voiced loud and

here's the money gone?" inquired

Molineux's seething South Bank choir en masse, before a half-time deputation of irate supporters made their feelings known face-to-face to man-aging director John Richards.

It was a mood of embittered annoyance even before Wycombe's fortunate early opener — an own goal from the helpless Kevin Muscat.

But the home faithful only really got a grasp of just how tough it would be when Steve Brown sent Jermaine McSporran clear to put Wycombe ahead in the tie for the first time.

And, even as Lee and his managerial assistant John Ward called the shots downstairs, Mr Richards was having to do some serious talking of his own as he bravely stood his ground in the directors

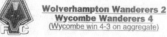
Wolverhampton Wanderers 2
Wycombe Wanderers 4
(Wycombe win 4-3 on aggregate)

box to address a clutch of angry supporters.

Haavard Flo nearly had Wolves back in it with a header from Andy Simton's corner which took Martin Taylor two attempts to save. But, within two min-utes, McSporran had made up for his first-half miss to turn and hoist the most outrageously looping lob high into the Molineux sky, up over Mike Stowell and into the net.

With the stunned crowd by now whipped up into a frenzied explosion of frustration, there had to be a sting in the tail. And with the front two of Flo and

Steve Corica made the scapegoats by having their numbers held aloft, it came. First through young Irish debutant Colin Larkin, who almost broke the net with his right-foot volley, soon after he had come on as sub. Then almost again when the typically battling Neil Emblen wriggled through, only for Taylor to bravely block.

But, when Wycombe skipper Keith Ryan powered in to bullet home Dave Carroll's header, it was the cue for half the disaffected home fans to stream for the exit. And a lot would not only have missed Emblen's latching onto Lee Naylor's cross to pull one back, but the subsequent agonising close shave from the big stopper that would have taken the tie to extra-time.

"I always thought it was going our night," insisted the distincti gant Wycombe boss, former Wim striker Lawrie Sanchez.

But Lee's own assessment night's events was more per "Good teams bounce back fro performances," he warned.

On Saturday, Molineux, an Graydon's Walsall, should find o good, or bad, Wolves are.

Scorers: Muscat og (10) 0-1; McSporran McSporran (59) 0-3; Larkin (72) 1-3; Ryan (l Emblen (89) 2-4

WOLVES (4-4-2): Stowell, Muscat, N Emb Naylor, Bazeley, Robinson, Sedgley, Simp Simpson 65), Corica (Larkin 64). Subs: Mast Green, Andrews.

WYCOMBE (3-4-3): Taylor, Cousins, Bate Lawrence, Ryan (P Emblen 88), Holsgrove (E Carroll, Devine (Baird 70), McSporran. Sub Harkin.

Bookings: Wolves - Naylor (foul); Wycombe McSporran (foul), Brown (late tackle)

Attendance: 13,723

Referee: M Pike (Barrow)

Wolves man of the match: Neil Emblen the end.

What a contrast just over three months later when Wolves beat First Division leaders Manchester City 4-1 to warm the hearts on a cold December evening.

Wolves sink City slickers

Wolves re-ignited their play-off challenge with their best win for more than a year at Molineux last night.

The players celebrated manager Colin Lee's 50th game in charge with a 4-1 win over the league leaders – Wolves biggest victory since a 6-1 demolition of Bristol City in Lee's first game as manager last season, *writes Malcolm Cinnamond.*

Two goals from on-loan Merseysider Michael Branch, one from Ade Akinbiyi and a fourth from Kevin Muscat were the crowning moments of an excellent all-round performance.

Akinbiyi opened the scoring after only six minutes, heading home from close range after Neil Emblen's header had been touched onto the bar by Nicky Weaver.

With City's defence having a nightmare evening, Branch followed that up 13 minutes later when he received a pass from Sinton, moved across the penalty area and whipped a shot past Weaver and into the net.

Shaun Goater gave City some respite when he scrambled Mark Kennedy's low, hard cross into the area, but Branch put Wolves back in control when he stretched out to convert a terrific cross by Akinbiyi.

Wolves sealed a cracking win midway through the second half when Kevin Muscat ran onto Darren Bazeley's cross to score his first of the season

City's £1.5m new striker Robert Taylor had three good chances to score. He hit the bar with one shot, had a fierce free-kick well saved by Wolves goalkeeper Michael Oakes and sent a second-half shot over the bar.

Wolves: Oakes; Muscat, Curle, Pollet, Naylor; Bazeley, Emblen, Osborn, Sinton (Scott Taylor 90+1); Branch (Corica, 84), Akinbiyi. **Subs:** Stowell, Robinson, Sedgley.

Booked: Pollet (45+1, foul on Taylor); **Osborn** (75, foul on Bishop).

Manchester City: Weaver; Edghill, Wiekens, Jobson, Granville (Tiatto, 55); Jeff Whitley (Pollock, 55); Horlock, Bishop, Kennedy; Goater, Robert Taylor. **Subs:** Crooks, Gareth Taylor, Wright.

Booked: Pollock (57, mistimed tackle on Emblen).

Referee: Steve Bennett (Orpington) **Attendance:** 21,635.

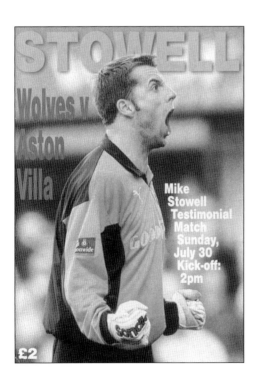

Just a fortnight earlier, goalkeeper Mike Stowell had played the last of his 447 games for Wolves – a record for a Wolves goalkeeper – before his well-earned benefit match against Aston Villa in July 2000. He had made his Wolves debut in a 4-0 win over Bury in March 1989 as the team roared towards promotion from the Third Division and he had kept over 100 clean sheets and saved countless penalties by the time he left Molineux. After one last substitute appearance at QPR in May 2001, Mike moved to Bristol City, with Michael Oakes holding down the goalkeeping spot at Wolves and making his 100th appearance during the 2000/01 season.

May 2001 saw many older Wolves fans in St Peter's church for a memorial service in honour of the late great Stan Cullis, who had died in February at the age of eighty-four. Eighty-one-year-old Bert Williams gave a most moving tribute to a man whom he had known as an opponent, a team-mate and a manager, and people of various faiths (and none) shared in a most moving occasion that reminded them that memories are eternal and football generates many of those.

Bert was just one of many players over the years to play for both Wolves and Walsall. Like Johnny Hancocks and Dennis Wilshaw, he moved from Walsall to Wolves just after the war, and went on to play for England.

Many more players have moved from Wolves to Walsall over the years and one of the most recent of these is Darren Bazeley, who moved from Watford to Wolves 1999 and played in all 51 League and Cup games for Wolves in 1999/2000. After injury problems in 2001/02, he moved to Walsall in the summer or 2002.

When Wolves beat Gillingham 2-0 on 7 March 2002, promotion to the Premiership seemed only a whisker away. 25,908 saw Alex Rae and Nathan Blake get the goals that left Wolves 8 points clear of second-place Manchester City and 10 points clear of West Brom in third. Alas just 10 points from the last 9 games and an inspired late run by West Brom cost Wolves automatic promotion and a play-off defeat by Norwich City did the rest. Now all that matters to Wolves is that the sort of form that earned them seven successive wins early in the year 2002 will be repeated in the following campaign. In the photograph, Kevin Muscat congratulates Alex Rae just a few games before his own move to Glasgow Rangers.

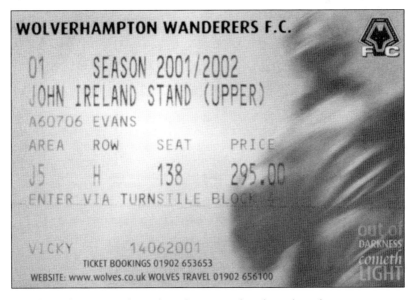

It costs more these days to watch Wolves than it used to, but when the team is on song fans feel that it is money well spent.

Sir Jack Hayward, who has been an avid Wolves fan since before the Second World War, is a supreme benefactor. Born in Dunstall a few yards from Molineux in 1923, Sir Jack was knighted in 1986 and took over Wolves in 1991. Since that time he has spent many millions of pounds on providing Wolves with one of the finest stadia in the country and a team that is surely on the edge of recapturing former glories.

 WOLVERHAMPTON WANDERERS F.C.
The Molineux Stadium

This is the house that Jack built. The magnificent new Molineux Stadium bears no resemblance to the rather derelict site of the 1980s. Wolves fans now wonder whether in due course the ground will be completed by having the corners filled in so that there will be room for 50,000 fans to watch Wolves when they reach the Premiership.